FUNCTIONAL TRAINING
FOR SPORTS

MICHAEL BOYLE

HUMAN KINETICS

Library of Congress Cataloging-in-Publication Data

Boyle, Michael, 1959-
   Functional training for sports / Michael Boyle.
      p. cm.
Includes bibliographical references (p.   ) and index.
   ISBN 0-7360-4681-X (soft cover)
   1. Athletes--Training of.   2. Physical education and training.   3.
Exercise.   I. Title.
   GV711.5.B69 2003
   613.7'11--dc21

                              2003008763

ISBN: 0-7360-4681-X

Copyright © 2004 by Michael Boyle

Acquisitions Editor: Ed McNeely; **Developmental Editor:** Laura Hambly; **Assistant Editor:** Alisha Jeddeloh; **Copyeditor:** Karen Bojda; **Proofreader:** Bob Replinger; **Indexer:** Bobbi Swanson; **Graphic Designer:** Nancy Rasmus; **Graphic Artist:** Sandra Meier; **Art and Photo Manager:** Dan Wendt; **Cover Designer:** Keith Blomberg; **Photographer (cover and interior):** Gary Land, unless otherwise noted; **Illustrator:** Mic Greenberg; **Printer:** United Graphics

Human Kinetics books are available at special discounts for bulk purchase. Special editions or book excerpts can also be created to specification. For details, contact the Special Sales Manager at Human Kinetics.

Printed in the United States of America

10   9   8   7   6   5   4   3   2   1

Human Kinetics
Web site: www.HumanKinetics.com

United States: Human Kinetics
P.O. Box 5076, Champaign, IL 61825-5076
800-747-4457
e-mail: humank@hkusa.com

Canada: Human Kinetics
475 Devonshire Road Unit 100, Windsor, ON N8Y 2L5
800-465-7301 (in Canada only)
e-mail: orders@hkcanada.com

Europe: Human Kinetics
107 Bradford Road, Stanningley, Leeds LS28 6AT, United Kingdom
+44 (0) 113 255 5665
e-mail: hk@hkeurope.com

Australia: Human Kinetics
57A Price Avenue, Lower Mitcham, South Australia 5062
08 8277 1555
e-mail: liahka@senet.com.au

New Zealand: Human Kinetics
P.O. Box 105-231, Auckland Central
09-523-3462
e-mail: hkp@ihug.co.nz

To Cindy and Michaela
for allowing me to fall in love twice.

contents

preface

As the use of functional training programs has proliferated, an obvious need has developed for a simple text that can be read and used by diverse people. Coaches, athletes, personal trainers, athletic trainers, physical therapists, and even concerned parents need an easy-to-read text that can simplify this complex topic. Because it has been stripped of buzzwords and scientific language, *Functional Training for Sports* will make sense to all these groups. Functional training is a purposeful system of programs and exercises to develop a higher level of athletic preparation. It is a system of preparation based not only on the latest scientific research but also on over 20 years of experience and hundreds of thousands of workouts. Functional training is not just about getting stronger or bigger; it is about reducing injuries and improving performance. Functional training focuses on injury reduction through the use of progressively more demanding exercises, and at the same time on performance enhancement. It is not a trend or a fad but rather the outgrowth of increased knowledge in the areas of rehabilitation and training. Functional training is the logical future of the field of performance enhancement.

In functional training, strength is developed with the intent of improving sport skills, not for the sake of more strength. Size is developed in areas that will benefit from greater size, not for aesthetics. Although many coaches glorify strength and flaunt the one-rep max of their athletes, strength should be judged with the knowledge that the only valuable strength is functional strength. Although many people train for appearance, functional training views improved appearance as a by-product of performance enhancement training.

Most articles and books on functional training are written by high-level coaches for high-level coaches. Although this text will prove useful to the high-level coach, the intended audience is less familiar with the topic of functional training. The book covers the spectrum from warm-up through strength development to sport conditioning in an easy-to-read and easy-to-follow format. The book speaks to high school coaches and high school athletic trainers in language that educates them. The information is detailed enough to be of use to physical therapists but also simple enough to be read by athletes and parents.

The book is organized in a simple fashion. The initial chapters provide background on the development of functional training and the rationale behind its use. Subsequent chapters describe the methods used in a functional training program by body region. Chapters include functional lower-body training, functional training for the torso, functional upper-body training, as well as chapters on plyometric training and Olympic lifting. Since a picture is worth a thousand words, photographs show the key positions of each functional training exercise described in these chapters.

The last chapter of the book details programs that incorporate the exercises and methods illustrated in the preceding chapters. It organizes these programs not only by sport type but also by training period (in-season or off-season) and by number of days required (two-day, three-day, or four-day programs). The last chapter alone makes the book valuable to coaches and athletes at both the high school and college level. You get sample in-season and off-season programs that involve minimal expense yet yield excellent results.

The book intentionally avoids complex anatomical or physiological descriptions except where absolutely necessary. When anatomical or physiological explanations are necessary, analogies and illustrations help simplify the concepts. The intention of the book is to educate the reader without causing confusion. The focus is on documenting progressions for each body region, moving from simple exercises to complex exercises.

Functional Training for Sports provides one-stop shopping for a total-body training program. You can begin with the warm-up, move on to power development, and progress to strength in an easy-to-follow format that is based on the concepts of mastery and progression. You are encouraged to master a skill before progressing and are continually reminded that what matters is mastering the skills. Phases of training are never shorter than three weeks, no matter your ability.

This book is unique in the sense that it is one of the first books on functional training written for the general public. One of the hardest things to do either in a presentation or in print is to make a complex topic appear simple. This book does just that. The book is written in a way that educates the novice but is not so simple that it is not worthwhile for the experienced coach or trainer. Athletes and coaches who read this book can expect to see significant improvements in performance if they follow the outlined progressions. In addition they will be able to assess their strengths and weaknesses more objectively and take the necessary action to make lasting changes. This book does not offer a quick fix or a gimmick but an organized system of training that will yield great results.

acknowledgments

It is a wonderful thing to have the opportunity to thank people who influence you and make your life enjoyable. I have the chance to work in a training utopia. We work with people we know and love and make the rules up as we go along. This work is the product of over 20 years of interaction between coach and athlete. To thank all those who had a hand in it would be a book in itself, but I will try to mention as many by name as I can.

The first people to thank are people I thought of often during the writing of this book: my parents, Arthur and Peg Boyle, who gave me books and taught me to read, and my junior high English teacher, Ms. Bothwell, who I was lucky enough to have for two years. I wrote this book because you taught me to write, a skill I didn't think would come in a handy when I started coaching.

I also thank my "teachers," many who taught me what to do and some who taught me who I wanted to be: Jack Parker, Mike Woicek, Vern Gambetta, Johnny Parker, Mimi Murray, Charlie Redmond, and many others.

I thank my colleagues, the people I look to for ideas: Mark Verstegen, Al Vermeil, Mike Clark, and Daryl Eto.

Chris Porier of Perform Better is a guy who thought that I had a talent and encouraged me and enabled me to speak. Chris is the reason people believe that I'm an expert and qualified to write this book.

Most important, I thank my coworkers: Walter Norton, Jr., a coach's coach and maybe the best coach I have ever been associated with; Bob Hanson, whose job it is to keep me sane in a sometimes insane business; Ed Lippie, Ed Mantie, Tricia Quagrello, and Karen Wood, who have supported and developed our business for the last five years. We could not and cannot do it without them. Steve Bunker, Kristen McCormick, Keri Herbert, Tricia Dunn, Katie King, and Michelle Sturgeon continue to allow us to get better every day.

Thanks to the folks at Reebok. Steve Gallo has been both an advisor and a friend. Kathy O'Connell and Michelle Pytko continue to help us and were instrumental in the process of creating the photographs for the book. Gary Land is not only talented but fun to work with. His photos would make a great book without any words and may set the standard for these books. Our Reebok® models, Rico Wesley and Umi Lee, provided excellent examples throughout the book.

Thanks to the folks at Human Kinetics for asking me to do something I have always wanted to do but probably wouldn't have done: Ed McNeely for guiding me through the process and Laura Hambly for her editing expertise.

Last, I thank the thousands of athletes from junior high to the professional level who have given all of us the chance to do what we love to do in an environment that is unparalleled in our industry.

ADDING FUNCTIONALITY TO YOUR PROGRAM

Function is, essentially, purpose. Functional training can therefore be described as purposeful training. Functional training has been mislabeled by many athletes and coaches as "sport specific," which implies that certain movements and movement patterns are specific to individual sports. In fact, functional training is more accurately represented as "sports-general" training. The "sports-general" school of thought views most sports as far more similar than different. Actions such as sprinting, striking, jumping, and moving laterally are general skills that apply to many sports. For example, a sports generalist believes that speed training for football and baseball are similar, as is torso training for golf, hockey, and tennis. Functional training looks at the commonalities of sport and reinforces them.

To refine the definition, ask yourself a few simple questions. How many sports are played sitting down? As far as I can tell, only a few sports, such as rowing, are performed from a seated position. Therefore, training muscles in a seated position is not functional for most sports. Second, how many sports are played in a rigid environment where stability is provided by outside sources? The answer to the second question would appear to be none. Most sports are contested on fields or courts. The stability is provided by the athlete, not by some outside source. Reasoning again tells us that most machine-based training systems are not by definition functional because the load is stabilized for the lifter by the machine. Proponents of machine-based training systems argue that machine-based training is safer, but there is a clear trade-off. Although machine-based training may result in fewer injuries in training, the lack of proprioceptive input (internal sensory feedback about position and movement) and the lack of stabilization will more than likely lead to a greater number of injuries during competition.

Another question to ask is, How many sport skills are performed by one joint acting in isolation? Again, the answer is zero. Functional training attempts to focus on multijoint movement as much as possible. Vern Gambetta and Gary Gray, two recognized experts on functional training, state, "Single joint movements that isolate a specific muscle are very non functional. Multi-joint movements which integrate muscle groups into movement patterns are very functional" (Gambetta and Gray 2002, paragraph 13). The number one goal of strength and conditioning professionals is injury reduction. If coaches employ a system of training that results in few training injuries but does not reduce competitive injuries, are they doing their job or protecting their job?

Most coaches would agree that functional training is best characterized by exercises done with the feet in contact with the ground and without the aid of machines. As you will see, there are always exceptions to the rules. What is paramount is that functional training is training with a purpose, training that makes sense.

Functional training prepares an athlete for his or her sport. It does not use one sport to train an athlete for another sport. Many collegiate strength programs are based on this premise. Functional training uses many concepts developed to improve speed, strength, and power to improve sport performance and reduce incidence of injury. The reason behind the functional training revolution can be found in the preceding definition of functional training. Functional training makes sense—not only to coaches but also to athletes.

In its simplest form, functional training teaches athletes how to handle their own body weight. The coach uses body weight as resistance and attempts to employ positions that make sense to the participant. Functional training intentionally incorporates balance and proprioception (body awareness) into training. Gambetta and Gray (2002, paragraph 8) state, "Functional training programs need to introduce controlled amounts

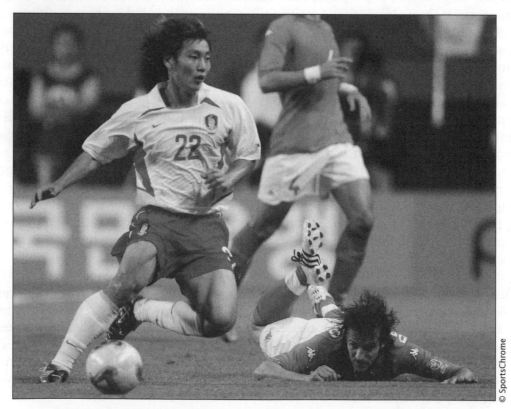

© SportsChrome

Functional training helps develop the strength and balance needed to perform on unstable surfaces such as grass and artificial turf.

of instability so that the athlete must react in order to regain their own stability." By design, functional training progresses to single-leg movements that require balance and to these movements performed with gradually increasing instability. Surfaces such as grass, artificial turf, or ice do not provide a consistent, stable platform on which to perform. The ability to display strength in conditions of instability is actually the highest expression of strength.

Functional training is a system that encourages the training of balance and the balancing of training. It is characterized by actions such as squatting and lunging or pushing and pulling. Functional training is best described as a continuum of exercises that teach athletes to handle their own body weight in all planes of movement. Experts emphasize that functional training trains *movements, not muscles.* There is no emphasis on overdeveloping strength in a particular movement; instead, emphasis is on attaining a balance between pushing and pulling strength and between knee-dominant hip extension (quadriceps and gluteals) and hip-dominant hip extension (hamstrings and gluteals).

The Science Behind Functional Training

To truly grasp the concept of functional training, it is necessary to accept a new paradigm to explain movement. This new paradigm was first introduced by physical therapist Gary Gray in his Chain Reaction courses in the 1990s. Gray promoted a new view of muscle function based not on the old definitions of flexion, extension, adduction, and abduction but on new views of kinetic chains. In the past, anatomy taught how a muscle moves an isolated joint, and no thought was given to what the muscle does in actual locomotion. In contrast, the concept of kinetic chains describes interrelated groups of joints and muscles working together to perform movements.

In simplest terms, Gray described the function of the lower extremity during locomotion as follows. When the foot hits the ground, every muscle from the trunk down has one simple function. The muscles of the lower body (glutes, quads, hamstrings) all act together to stop the ankle, knee, and hip from bending in order to prevent falling to the ground. In Gray's terms, all of the muscles have the same function. The muscles act to decelerate or slow down flexion at the ankle, knee, and hip. This concept is a tough one to swallow initially, but upon further review, it makes sense. In landing, is the quadriceps a knee extensor? No, the quadriceps is actually contracting eccentrically to prevent knee flexion. Is the hamstring a knee flexor? The hamstring in fact is acting in a dual role to prevent both knee flexion and hip flexion. As you think this through, the answer becomes more obvious and correspondingly easier to accept. In the landing phase of running, all the muscles of the lower extremity act in concert to prevent an action, not to cause one. All the muscles eccentrically (by lengthening) decelerate, or slow down, flexion at the ankle, knee, and hip.

Once you've grasped the preceding concept, the next step comes more simply. You should now understand that after the athlete has placed the foot on the ground and decelerated flexion, all the lower-extremity muscles again act as a unit to initiate extension at the ankle, knee, and hip. In fact, the quadriceps is not just extending the knee but assisting with plantar flexion of the ankle and extension of the hip. All the muscles act eccentrically in the first sequence to stop a movement and then milliseconds later act concentrically to create a movement. If these concepts begin to make sense, you are on your way to understanding the underlying science of functional training. When an athlete performs a leg extension, he or she is using a muscle action and nervous system pattern that are never employed when walking or running. The athlete is by definition performing *open-chain* muscle action. *Open-chain* means that the foot is not in contact with the ground (or a stable platform). To exercise a muscle as it will be used, you need to close the chain and allow the muscles to work as they would when the foot is on the ground. In regard to the lower extremity, *open-chain* or *single-joint* can be considered almost synonymous with *nonfunctional*.

The Functional Controversy

Over the past 10 years, there has been a shift toward making training more functional. The revolution began, as it often does, with physical therapists, and functional training was slowly adopted by coaches and personal trainers. One of the many signs that functional training would be the wave of the future was when the large manufacturers of strength-training machines began to introduce what they called "ground-based" machines and also to manufacture basic squat racks and weight benches. At this point the handwriting was on the wall. The public had spoken with their wallets, and the popularity of machines, particularly in the athletic training area, was on the decline.

However, over the past few years, a controversy has begun to develop around functional training. A kind of functional paradox has arisen. The gurus of functional training seem to deliver a clear message: Functional training should be done standing and should be multijoint. Surprisingly, however, some coaches who have embraced functional training espouse concepts that, in the initial analysis, appear nonfunctional. This use of apparently nonfunctional exercises by supposed proponents of functional training caused some confusion in the field. The reasoning behind this apparent contradiction is actually simple. Function varies from joint to joint. Exercises that promote the function of joints that require stabilization are different from exercises that promote the function of joints that strive for mobility. The primary function of certain muscles and muscle groups is stabilization. Functional training for those muscles involves training them to be better stabilizers, often by performing simple exercises through small ranges of motion. In many cases, in the effort to make everything functional, coaches and athletes ended up neglecting the important stabilizing functions of certain muscle groups.

The three key groups in need of stability training are

1. the deep abdominals (transversus abdominis and internal oblique),
2. the hip abductors and rotators, and
3. the scapula stabilizers.

Many coaches began to label exercises for these areas as rehabilitative or "prehabilitative," but in fact, these exercises are just another form of functional training. Function at the ankle, knee, and hip is maximized when the hip displays great stability. For some athletes the development of stability at the hip may initially require isolated hip abduction work to properly "turn on," or activate, the muscle. Performance expert Mark Verstegen of Athletes' Performance Institute in Tempe, Arizona, refers to this concept as "isolation for innervation." At certain times, certain muscle groups—notably the deep abdominals, hip abductors, and scapula stabilizers—need to be isolated to improve their function. For this reason, some single-joint, apparently nonfunctional exercises may in fact improve function of the entire lower extremity. This is one of the paradoxes of functional training.

Function at the shoulder joint is enhanced by improving the function of the scapula stabilizers. Although many athletes perform exercises for the rotator cuff, few exercise the scapula stabilizers. But a strong rotator cuff without strong scapula stabilizers is like trying to shoot a cannon from a canoe. At our training facility, we have found that most athletes have adequate rotator cuff strength but insufficient strength or control of the scapula stabilizers. As a result, we frequently employ exercises to work on the scapula stabilizers that might appear nonfunctional, but the development of these areas is critical to long-term health of the shoulder joint.

Physical therapists are again leading the way in the area of developing the stabilizers of the lower back. Improving abdominal strength to aid in the stabilization of the lower back is far from a new concept, but the specific methods are changing rapidly. Researchers in Australia have clearly established that two deep spinal stabilizing muscles, the transversus abdominis and multifidus, experience rapid atrophy after an episode of low-back pain. Without retraining these muscles, the recurrence of back pain is almost guaranteed. To improve the function of the lumbar spine, a certain degree of isolation is necessary, and this isolation involves simple, short-range contractions of the deep abdominal muscles.

The key to developing a truly functional training program is not to go too far in any particular direction. The majority of exercises should be done standing and should be multijoint, but at the same time, attention should be paid to development of the key stabilizer groups in the hips, torso, and posterior shoulder.

A second functional paradox revolves around multiplanar activity done in a sport-specific position. Advocates of this style of functional training espouse the use of loaded exercises (for example, dumbbell, weight vest) with a flexed posture and foot positions that some strength and conditioning coaches would consider less than desirable. Although athletes find themselves in compromised positions in competitive situations, coaches need to evaluate how far they are willing to go in loading athletes in positions of spinal flexion. As an example, although a baseball player often squats down to field a ground ball with a flexed spine, weighted squatting movements with the spine in a flexed position may not be wise. At what point do you cross the line from safe training into unsafe training? Our position on this is simple. The argument that "this happens in sports all the time" is not sufficient to take risks in the weight room. If we are training for strength (six reps or less), we never compromise back safety to make the body position of the exercise more specific. If we are training for endurance (10 reps or more), we *may* at times employ exercises in flexed postures while loaded with a weight vest or dumbbell. Physical therapist Mike Clark of the National Academy of Sports Medicine has proposed a guideline of not more than 10 percent of body weight for exercises done with a flexed spine or for forward-reaching actions. This is an excellent guide for most athletes but may be too heavy for larger athletes.

As you begin to explore the concept of functional training for sport, keep an open mind about how and why athletes move in your sport. Think of your training as a vehicle to improve performance, not just to improve strength. Many athletes have neglected strength training because they do not fully understand the performance-enhancing value of strength in sports such as baseball, tennis, or soccer. The key from the athlete's standpoint is for the training to make sense. The key from the coach's standpoint is to make the training make sense to the athlete. A training program built around actions that do not occur in sport simply does not make sense. The key is to design a training program that truly prepares athletes for their sports. This can be done only by using exercises that train the muscles the same way they are used in sport, in other words, functional training.

2

ANALYZING THE DEMANDS OF YOUR SPORT

Before you can design an effective functional training program, you must first analyze and understand the demands of your sport. Think about your sport. See a picture in your mind. What type of sport is it? Most sports are either endurance sports or speed and power sports. Almost all team sports are speed and power sports. Individual sports such as gymnastics and figure skating are also primarily speed and power sports. Racket sports, including tennis, are speed and power sports. Then ask yourself who the dominant players or performers are. Are they the athletes with the best endurance or the best flexibility? Most often that is not the case. Usually the best players or top performers are the most efficient and explosive movers. Speed and agility are the qualities prized in almost any speed and power sport.

Unfortunately, in the early 1980s when professional sports teams and top amateur and professional athletes began to seek advice on self-improvement, they often turned to the wrong people. Consultants employed by professional teams and top performers were most often exercise physiologists with little or no experience dealing with speed- and power-oriented athletes. Generally, they were endurance athletes themselves. The exercise physiologists employed in the '80s applied simple logic:

1. Test the players.
2. Analyze the tests.
3. Draw conclusions.

This seemed like a very simple method to address the complex task of improving athletes in all sports. However, this approach has a number of flaws, many of which continue to plague strength and conditioning professionals two decades later. Most athletes performed poorly on tests of steady-state aerobic capacity ($\dot{V}O_2$). Generally, these tests were performed for simplicity's sake on cycle ergometers by athletes who did not regularly train on a bike. The conclusions based on $\dot{V}O_2$ scores were that the athletes were unfit. The plan was to improve aerobic capacity, thereby improving the player. The rationale was that a player with a higher maximal oxygen uptake would be able to play longer and recover more rapidly. All of this seemed scientific and valid. However, there are a number of reasons that this approach does not meet the needs of athletes in speed and power sports:

■ Athletes in sports that use primarily fast-twitch muscles and explosive movements generally perform poorly on tests of aerobic capacity. This is not a new discovery. Seeking to "improve" these explosive athletes often is not as simple as it may seem.

■ Well-conditioned athletes in sports of an intermittent nature (i.e., most team sports) may not necessarily perform well in steady-state tests of aerobic capacity, particularly when the test is done on an apparatus (such as a bike) that is not the athlete's primary mode of training.

■ Steady-state or long-distance training to improve the fitness or aerobic capacity of fast and explosive athletes often detracts from the physiological qualities that make these athletes special.

■ Explosive athletes frequently develop overuse injuries when required to perform extensive amounts of steady-state work.

■ The technology used to improve aerobic capacity may in fact be the enemy. Lack of ground contact and lack of hip extension can set an athlete up for numerous injuries. Cyclists should ride bikes, rowers should row, athletes who have to run fast should run fast on the ground, and athletes who have to jump should jump.

Exercise physiologists looked at the problem from the wrong side. You don't simply analyze a top performer and seek to improve his weakness. What appears from one point of view to be a weakness may in fact be a strength. The improvement of perceived weaknesses can be like Delilah cutting off Samson's hair. By blindly attempting to improve what is perceived as a weakness, a coach in fact may be detracting from a strength. This is particularly applicable when training young people. When coaching young athletes, emphasis should be on the development of qualities such as speed and power over the development of fitness.

Identifying and Improving Key Qualities

Noted speed expert Charlie Francis wrote a landmark work in 1986 called *The Charlie Francis Training System* (reissued as *Training for Speed,* Francis 2000). In it he described the characteristics of a sprinter and how to properly train these characteristics. This information has been the basis for our program design and philosophy since that time. Francis coached Olympic champion Ben Johnson, and although Francis's coaching results are considered tainted, the accomplishments of Charlie Francis as a coach must not be understated. Canada was not considered a hotbed of sprinting, but Francis developed world-record holders in that cold climate without a huge population base. His athletes won gold medals at the Olympic Games, World Championships, and Commonwealth Games.

Francis came to simple and logical conclusions about developing sprinters. He believed that there must be sufficient power-related training during an athlete's early years (ages 13–17) to maintain the genetically determined level of white (fast-twitch or power-related) muscle fiber. Power-related work also promotes the shift of transitional fiber to power-related muscle fiber. Francis (2000) states, "Endurance work must be carefully limited to light-light/medium volumes to prevent the conversion of transitional or intermediate muscle fiber to red, endurance muscle fiber."

Francis believed that not only can you make an athlete into a sprinter but, more important, that you might negatively affect an athlete's ability to develop speed by focusing on endurance. In other words, it's easy to make a sprinter into an endurance athlete, but this is generally not a desirable result.

The key is to analyze a sport to ascertain the qualities that make a great performer and then to develop a program to improve those qualities. The key is not necessarily in analyzing a great performer and trying to improve what he does not do well. For years coaches have been trying to improve the aerobic capacity of explosive athletes. The end result seems to be an athlete with a higher oxygen uptake but no real change in performance. Training programs designed in this way improve the athlete's ability to work at a sustained pace in sports that do not require a sustained pace. The defenders of this practice point to the importance of the aerobic system to recovery and tell you things like "A soccer player runs five miles in a soccer match" or "A tennis match can last two hours." This point is not contestable. The question is, At what speed and in what time period? A tennis match may take two hours to play, but what is the ratio of sprinting to standing? Are the players in constant motion? The advocates of aerobic training never point to this training as a way to improve performance, only as away to improve recovery. The goal is to improve performance.

© Human Kinetics

Speed, power, and agility are important in sports like tennis, where players repeatedly accelerate and decelerate.

A soccer match is actually a series of sprints, jogs, and walks that occur over two hours. Any athlete can run five miles in two hours. In fact, most people can walk five miles in two hours. The important point is that great soccer players can accelerate and decelerate repeatedly during these two hours. Now ask yourself, "How do I condition for soccer?"

To train for sports such as soccer or tennis, you must sprint and decelerate, often from top speed, to be prepared to play the game. Will you develop this ability in five-mile runs? Probably not. The same logic can apply to almost any power sport. In football the athlete generally runs 10 yards or less. The plays take five seconds. There is almost 40 seconds of rest between plays. How should you condition for football? Probably with short sprints with 30- to 40-second rests. This is the key to analyzing your sport. Watch the game. Watch the great players. Look for the common denominators. Don't focus on what they can't do; try to figure out why the great ones do things well. Don't continue to accept what is viewed as common knowledge if it defies common sense.

To analyze your sport ask yourself a few questions:

- Does my sport require that I sprint or jump? If so, then lower-body strength (particularly the single-leg variety) is critical.

- How long is my event, or how long does a play last? (This is a bit complicated, but think about the total length of a game, program, or routine, or think about how long a rest you get between shifts, plays, or points.)

- Am I on the field, ice, track, or court the entire time?

- If I am, how often do I sprint, and how often do I jog? Do I jog for extended periods of time (over five minutes)? If not, than why do it in training?

- Do my speed and power place me in the top 10 percent of athletes in my sport? Male athletes: Can I complete the 10-yard dash in under 1.65 electronic? (*Electronic* refers to more accurate electronic timing rather than a handheld stopwatch.) Can I jump vertically over 34 inches? Female athletes: Can I complete the 10-yard dash in under 1.85 electronic? Can I jump vertically over 25 inches? If the answers are no, you can always use more speed and power.

Speed and power are essential for almost all sports. Tennis, soccer, baseball, gymnastics, figure skating, and other sports too numerous to mention all rely heavily on power and speed. The key to improving sport performance lies in improving the ability to produce speed and power. Endurance should be an afterthought. We tell our athletes over and over that it takes years to get fast and powerful and weeks to get in aerobic shape. With this in mind as you continue to read, begin to think about how you are currently training and how you might train smarter.

3

ASSESSING YOUR FUNCTIONAL STRENGTH

As stated in chapter 1, functional training is training that makes sense. After analyzing the demands of your sport, the next step is to take a brief inventory of yourself to assess your strengths and weaknesses. The tests in this chapter give you an opportunity to do some self-assessment.

It is rare to find an athlete who has too much strength or too much speed for his sport. You rarely hear a commentator say, "Boy, he was so fast he ran right by that ball." Think of strength as the road to speed and power. The key is to have functional strength, strength that you can use.

The assessment of functional strength is often humbling for even the best athletes. To assess functional strength, athletes must move a resistance, most frequently their own body, in an exercise that stresses the body in a way that might occur in sport. In most common strength-training tests, the athlete is asked to move a predetermined amount of weight in an exercise for which there are readily available norms. The bench press is often used to measure upper-body strength, but those who advocate the development of functional strength question the use of a test in which the athlete lies on the back. In most sports, lying on the back indicates a failure to perform at a high level. We tell our football players this: If you are lying on your back pushing up, you stink at football. Does this mean that you cannot bench-press in a functional program? No, you can use the bench press to develop general upper-body strength, but if you cannot perform body-weight exercises such as push-ups, chin-ups, and dips, then you are not functionally strong and may be more likely to be injured.

Remember, numbers can be deceiving. In most cases an athlete who can bench-press 350 pounds would be considered strong. What if the athlete weighs 350 pounds? The athlete can then bench-press only his own body weight. Don't be fooled by the number; athletes need to perform functional exercises with their body weight.

A good functional strength-training program is one that employs tried and true strength exercises such as the bench press and front squat and then transforms the strength developed into functional strength through movements such as stability ball push-ups and one-leg squats. Don't throw out the baby with the bathwater. Don't forsake methods that have been used successfully for 50 years to develop strength just to have a more functional program.

On the other side of the coin, don't develop strength just for strength's sake. The key to functional training is to develop appropriate levels of general strength and to utilize this strength in functional exercises. This training does not need to be an either/or proposition. Too often in the field of strength and conditioning, coaches attempt to adhere to one school of thought as opposed to developing appropriate training programs for their athletes. Athletes in training are not necessarily power lifters or Olympic lifters, so the objective should be to combine knowledge from a number of disciplines to provide the best training program possible.

Assessing Functional Upper-Body Strength

To assess functional upper-body strength, administer the following three simple tests.

1. *Maximum number of pull-ups (with palms forward) for males or chin-ups (palms toward the face) for females.* Elbows must be extended after each rep is completed, and the shoulder blades must abduct to produce visible movement (see figure 3.1). Don't count any reps not done to full extension or any reps in which the chin does get above the bar. Most athletes who claim to be able to do large numbers of pull-ups actually perform half pull-ups. Athletes who cannot do a pull-up or chin-up are not functionally strong and are more likely to be injured, particularly in the rotator cuff of the shoulder.

The following is a list of expectations for the number of pull-ups for men and chin-ups for women. Please note that these are realistic numbers based on our results with thousands of athletes using the testing technique described earlier. Any deviation greatly affects the test results. Most athletes take up to one year to achieve even the high school level if they have not regularly performed chin-ups. To improve, an athlete cannot follow a program of pull-downs. Assisted chin-ups and eccentric chin-ups (10- to 20-second lowerings only from the bar) must be done. Please refer to chapter 9 for detailed chin-up progressions.

Figure 3.1 Chin-up.

Pull-Ups and Chin-Ups

	Males (up to 225 pounds)	Females (up to 170 pounds)
World class	25+	15+
National caliber	20–25	10–15
Collegiate	15–20	5–10
High school	10–15	3–5
NFL linemen	8–10	

2. *Maximum number of inverted rows.* The inverted row is the reverse of the bench press and primarily works the scapula retractors, shoulder muscles involved in pulling movements. The athlete places the feet on a bench and grips a bar as if to perform a bench press. The bar should be set in a power rack at the height to which the athlete normally bench-presses. With the entire body held rigid, the athlete pulls the chest to the bar. The chest must touch the bar with no change in body position. Make sure that there is full extension of the elbow and that the body is kept perfectly straight. Count only the reps in which the chest touches the bar while the body remains straight (see figure 3.2).

If athletes cannot perform an inverted row, they lack upper-back strength and should begin with the level 1 rowing exercises described in chapter 9. An athlete who lacks upper-back strength is at greater risk for problems related to the shoulder's rotator cuff. This is of particular importance to athletes prone to rotator cuff problems such as swimmers, tennis players, pitchers, quarterbacks, and other throwing athletes.

Figure 3.2 Inverted row.

Inverted Rows

	Males (up to 225 pounds)	Females (up to 170 pounds)
World class	25+	15+
National caliber	20–25	10–15
Collegiate	15–20	5–10
High school	10–15	3–5
NFL linemen	8–10	

3. *Maximum number of push-ups.* This is a much more accurate test for larger athletes than bench press numbers. For each push-up, the nose should touch the ground and the torso should stay rigid. Do not count reps in which back position is not maintained, the nose does not touch the ground, or the elbows are not fully extended. To prevent cheating and make counting simple, use a metronome set at 50 beats per minute. The athlete should keep pace with the metronome, going up on the first beat and down on the next, to perform 25 push-ups per minute. The test is over when the athlete fails to do another push-up or cannot keep pace with the metronome.

Push-Ups

	Males (up to 225 pounds)	Females (up to 170 pounds)
World class	50	35
National caliber	42	27
Collegiate	35	20
High school	25	12

Assessing Functional Lower-Body Strength

The safe and accurate assessment of functional lower-body strength is significantly more difficult than the assessment of upper-body strength. Few reliable tests exist that safely measure functional lower-body strength. The one-leg box squat (see chapter 6) done with the foot on an Airex® mat is the best test of lower-body strength, but the one-leg squat done in this fashion is more accurately the best *demonstration* of lower-body strength. The one-leg box squat is not a reliable test because it is primarily a pass/fail test that initially tests experience and learning rather than actual strength. A valid, reliable, and safe test that is simple to administer really does not exist for the lower body. Assumptions can be based on the performance of different types of one-leg squats, but no standards have been established.

We have found that functionally strong athletes can perform sets of five one-leg squats with five-pound dumbbells in the hands by the beginning of the seventh week of a properly designed training program (see figure 3.3). Athletes unfamiliar with or unaccustomed to single-leg strength work should progress through three weeks of split squats (both feet on the floor) and three weeks of one-leg bench squats (back foot elevated) before attempting to perform one-leg squats.

Figure 3.3 One-leg box squat with five-pound dumbbells.

Other tests have been suggested, but their validity or reliability is questionable. It is nearly impossible to safely assess functional lower-body strength without first teaching the athlete the exercise. In this case, the risk outweighs the potential benefits.

A simple alternative is to use the two-leg vertical jump to assess leg power and then to reassess leg power after a proper strength program has been initiated. The vertical-jump test is relatively safe to administer and has readily available norms. Increases in leg power are at least partially attributable to increases in leg strength. The Just Jump System® and Vertec® are the best devices for evaluating the vertical jump, although both methods have inherent flaws. (Both devices are distributed by M-F Athletic Company and can be purchased at www.performbetter.com.) Just Jump is a device that measures time in the air and converts it to inches. The athlete must jump and land in the same place, and the athlete must land toes first with no knee lift or knee bend. All these factors influence the score. The Vertec is an adjustable device that measures both reach height and jump height. With the Vertec, the reach measurement must be accurate. At our training facility, we test a two-hand reach and a one-hand touch on the jump. Consistency among testers and in test administration is essential.

Two-Leg Vertical Jump (in inches)

	Males (up to 225 pounds)	Females (up to 170 pounds)
World class	35+	25+
National caliber	33–35	20–25
Collegiate	25–30	20
High school	22–25	15–20

It is important to understand that testing is done to evaluate progress. Tests are not the program and should not be the program. Testing shows what is needed and what areas may be prone to injury. Some coaches criticize this type of testing protocol because some of the tests can be construed as tests of muscular endurance. Although I agree, it must be stated again that the tests are not the training program, only a method of evaluating progress. In training, these numbers are used to aid in the development of strength. For example, the maximum number of chin-ups or pull-ups is used to determine the weights used for weighted pull-ups. For sets of five reps, athletes are instructed to begin with a weight that corresponds to the number of pull-ups or chin-ups they can perform. This simple method progresses movements that are often not progressed properly.

As a specific example, an athlete who can do 25 pull-ups would begin with sets of five weighted pull-ups with 25 pounds. For sets of three reps, athletes use 1.5 times the number of pull-ups, which would be 37 pounds for this athlete. Using this progression, we know female athletes who can perform three reps with 45 pounds and male athletes who use over 90 pounds for chin-ups.

The evaluation of functional strength is an important step in developing your training plan. At this point you should better understand the demands of your sport and have an idea about your strength level. Hopefully, the principles of functional training are becoming clearer to you. The idea is to develop a plan that makes sense for your sport and strengthens areas that are key to performance or to injury prevention. The next step is to begin to develop the plan.

When testing functional strength, technique counts. The world is full of people touting inflated scores based on questionable testing methods. Think of these words from the famous anthropologist Margaret Mead, "What people say, what people do, and what they say they do are entirely different things." Be an athlete or a coach who "walks the walk." Don't test for ego inflation or to impress others; test tough to evaluate progress. You will gain the respect of athletes and peers.

4

DESIGNING YOUR PROGRAM

The next step in designing a functional training program is to understand the underlying concepts of program design. This chapter will familiarize you with the concepts and the tools used to implement the concepts and to progress in the program. The emphasis is on not only improving strength but incorporating balance and stabilization with strength.

Designing a functional exercise program can be both fun and challenging. The amount of information can be daunting and the recommendations confusing. To simplify, review the basics of chapter 2:

- Is your sport a sprint-dominated sport that emphasizes speed and power?
- Are you required to stop and start frequently?
- How long does a play, point, shift, or routine last?

One thing you should realize is that almost every team sport is a sprint-dominated sport in which players stop and start frequently. As a result, most or all of the conditioning after a two- to three-week preparatory period should be primarily stop-and-start conditioning similar in concept to the 300-yard shuttle run. The preparatory period should consist of extensive tempo running to develop a base of sprint-related conditioning. Extensive tempo running is neither sprinting nor jogging. It consists of runs of various distances (generally 100 or 200 yards) interspersed with walking recovery. At our training facility, athletes frequently stride the length of a football field and walk the width. ("Stride" is literally the middle ground between jogging and sprinting.)

Soccer, field hockey, lacrosse, basketball, tennis, and ice hockey are all sprint-dominated sports in which athletes stop and start frequently. After analyzing what actually happens in a game, attempt to mimic the energy systems and style of the game. Many coaches have advocated Fartlek training, a system of conditioning in which the athlete intersperses periods of jogging with periods of higher speed running. However, I strongly believe that it is too easy to cheat in Fartlek training. Fartlek training becomes just more long-distance aerobic work for most athletes. Athletes need to be told how far to run, how fast, and how much rest to take between runs. Athletes allowed to run at their own pace most often run too slowly. Athletes allowed to control their rest most often rest too long.

Principles of Program Design

To properly design a functional strength training program, keep the following principles in mind.

- *Learn the basic exercises first.* Master the basics before considering progressions such as unstable-surface training on a stability ball, foam roller, or Airex pad. The biggest mistake in attempting to make an exercise program more functional is for athletes who are not competent in a basic movement, such as the squat, to attempt that movement on an unstable surface. Learn to do a body-weight squat; learn to do a proper push-up; learn to do a chin-up. Then and only then should you follow the recommended progressions.

- *Begin with simple body-weight exercises.* The number one way to mess up a strength program is by attempting to lift too much weight. If an athlete can perform an exercise with body weight but struggles with an external load, then the external load is the problem. Either reduce or eliminate the external load. For upper-body pulling or rowing movements, many athletes are unable to begin with even body-weight resistance. In this case, machines or elastic assistance may be necessary.

- *Progress from simple to complex.* The progressions in this book were developed over many years. Follow these progressions. For single-leg exercises, master the simplest exercise, such as the split squat, before progressing to a more complex exercise such as the one-leg bench squat. The exercises follow a functional progression and add surface instability at the appropriate time as needed.

For body-weight exercise, the progression is simple. Begin with three sets of 8 repetitions in week 1, move to three sets of 10 in week 2, and three sets of 12 in week 3. This is simple overload training. If you do not want to add repetitions, add external resistance.

By the fourth week, you can progress to a more difficult exercise. The more difficult exercise can then be progressed by the same method, or basic resistance progression can be employed. The best way for beginners to become strong is simple, progressive resistance. Adding 5 pounds per week to an exercise results in an increase of 260 pounds per year. Most athletes dream about gains like this, and in reality, most athletes eventually plateau on this type of program, but beginners can progress for a long time with basic resistance progression.

One word of caution in program design: Don't design a program based on what you like or dislike; design a program that works for the athlete. Coaches and trainers often inadvertently bias their programs based on their own personal tastes. This error should be avoided.

Functional Training Tools

Many coaches and athletes seem to think that functional training consists of cute exercises done with stability balls. This could not be further from the truth. True functional training begins with the ultimate tool: body weight. Athletes should be able to master skills with body weight before adding any instability. Although unstable-surface training, as on a stability ball, provides additional stress to the stabilizer muscles, most athletes need time to develop the stability necessary to perform many exercises on a stable surface first. Watch a novice attempt to split-squat with just his or her body weight; the lack of balance is evident. No additional instability is needed in most cases. Following are a brief overview of functional training equipment and some guidelines for how and when to use it.

Stability Balls. The stability ball has unfortunately become synonymous with functional training. Books have been written, videos made, and classes developed around the stability ball. The overuse of the stability ball alone has caused many strength and conditioning coaches to view functional training negatively. Coaches and athletes need to remember that the stability ball is simply one type of unstable surface and may be inappropriate for many beginning trainees. The stability ball is an excellent tool for adding instability to torso stabilization exercises or upper-body exercises such as push-ups (see figure 4.1). In addition, the stability ball can be used for numerous glute and hamstring exercises.

What the stability ball is not, however, is a tool for squatting or for lifting loads heavier than body weight. Videos showing athletes standing on a ball are potentially negligent. Athletes should never stand on a stability ball. The risks far outweigh any potential benefits. If you desire an unstable surface for additional balance training for the lower extremity, use another tool.

Coaches and athletes should also be cautious about sitting on a stability ball during barbell or dumbbell exercises or using the stability ball as a bench for pressing movements. Stability balls that are not burst resistant should never be used for support with

Figure 4.1 Stability ball push-up.

dumbbells or a bar, as these balls will not deflate but instead will burst if punctured. Caution should also be used with burst-resistant balls. There have been reports of burst-resistant balls tearing in the same manner as conventional balls and causing serious injury. Our current policy is body weight only and no standing on stability balls due to safety concerns.

Half Foam Roller. Another valuable piece of functional training equipment is a 12-inch half foam roller. The half foam roller can introduce a moderately unstable surface with a minimum amount of risk to most single-leg exercises. The half foam roller is rounded on top but conforms somewhat to the shape of the foot. The half foam roller elevates the trainee only slightly, and the rounded top stimulates the ankle, knee, and hip to generate greater stabilization forces. The half foam roller can be used to increase the balancing challenge of almost any single-leg exercise but provides primarily frontal plane instability (see figure 4.2).

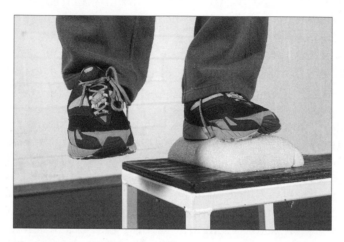

Figure 4.2 Half foam roller.

Airex® Mats. An Airex mat is the next progression in instability after the half foam roller. Such mats are more three-dimensionally unstable and therefore provide a multi-plane challenge to the lower extremity. Athletes progress from exercises performed on a solid surface to the two-dimensional instability of the half foam roller and eventually to the three-dimensional instability of the mat. The ultimate expression of strength with stability is the one-leg squat on an Airex mat (see figure 3.3 on page 15).

Reebok® Core Board. The Reebok Core Board is an excellent addition to the functional training equipment list. The Core Board was developed for Reebok by physical therapist Alex McKechnie. Simply put, the Core Board is a three-dimensionally unstable balance platform that can respond dynamically to the athlete's movements or simply function as a balance board, depending on the demand. Unlike a simple balance board, the Core Board can respond to a movement. For example, if you shift your weight to one side, the board exerts a force that pushes you back in the opposite direction. This forces the muscles to cope with the response. Exercises can be done with three-dimensional instability and with concentric and eccentric movement (see figure 4.3). The Core Board is an essential piece of equipment in all strength and conditioning, physical therapy, and athletic training settings.

Figure 4.3   Reebok Core Board.

Slide Board.   The slide board was initially developed as a training device for speedskaters but has gained widespread use in other sports. The slide board is the only piece of equipment that can provide energy system and muscular system work in a sport-specific position. The slide board allows the athlete to perform energy system work while standing and, by its nature, forces athletes to assume the bent-knee posture that has been dubbed the sport-specific position (see figure 4.4). Athletes can develop conditioning while also developing appropriate muscle patterns, something that is usually not possible on a conventional piece of cardiovascular equipment. The slide board allows the athlete to work all of the extensor muscles of the lower body as well as the hip abductors and adductors. From a functional conditioning standpoint, the benefits of the slide board may be equal to or better than running. At our training facility, we require all our athletes to use the slide board, as it can enhance lateral movement and balance while also conditioning the difficult-to-train hip abductor and adductor muscle groups. No other piece of energy system conditioning equipment can provide all these benefits. In addition, the slide board can easily accommodate users of various heights and weights.

Figure 4.4   Slide board.

Agility Ladder. The agility ladder may be one of the best pieces of functional training equipment available. The agility ladder allows a dynamic warm-up that can emphasize any number of components. The agility ladder can be used to develop balance, foot speed, coordination, or eccentric strength (see figure 4.5). Until the advent of the agility ladder, there was not a good way to work on foot speed. The agility ladder provides benefits to both the muscular system and the neuromuscular system while increasing muscle temperature.

Fitter®. The Fitter was initially developed in Canada for ski training but is an excellent addition to the functional training toolbox. The Fitter is a system that consists of a moving top piece (the skate) and a fixed bottom (the base). The skate has a wheeled bottom and is attached to the base via adjustable and interchangeable elastic cords of various thicknesses that allow the skate to glide over the base (see figure 4.6). The Fitter allows the athlete to perform numerous lateral, linear, and diagonal movement patterns with both the upper and lower body for balance, torso strength, upper-body strength, and lower-body strength. For rehabilitation, the Fitter can be used to develop stability with movement in almost any joint.

Figure 4.5 Agility ladder.

Figure 4.6 Fitter.

Medicine Balls. The medicine ball is the best tool for functional training of the torso and prevention of rotator cuff injury. Although medicine balls have been around for centuries, rubber and nonlatex medicine balls with rebound capability have become tools of the future. The medicine ball can be used for upper-body power work through exercises such as chest passes and can be thrown for distance for total-body power work. An entire section on training with the medicine ball is included in chapter 8. The medicine ball combined with a masonry wall is a wonderful tool to elicit a plyometric effect. Care must be taken to avoid injury with the medicine ball. Athletes at our training facility do not perform many partner drills that require catching the ball, nor do they perform single-arm overhead movements. Catching the ball can result in hand injury, while single-arm overhead activities may be too stressful on the shoulder joint.

Weight Vests. Some coaches think that a weight vest is redundant if athletes are already training with bars or dumbbells. In fact, the weight vest adds an external load with minimal disruption of the movement of the body. Athletes do not need to change the position of the upper body to hold an external load; they simply need to put on weight vests. The weight vest is an excellent way to add additional resistance to body-weight exercises such as the push-up, body-weight squat, and inverted row. In addition, for sports such as ice hockey and football, the weight vest allows athletes to simulate the weight of additional equipment during conditioning workouts.

The Functional Continuum

The functional continuum (figure 4.7) rates some exercises from least functional to most functional. The exercises are grouped into lower-body exercises (both knee dominant and hip dominant), upper-body exercises (both pushing and pulling), and torso exercises. The figure demonstrates the progression from relatively nonfunctional, often machine-based exercises to highly functional exercises on an unstable surface. You must always combine some basic strength exercises that are less functional with exercises that are higher on the functional continuum. The program is never an either/or program but rather an integrated approach of developing strength and making that strength more relevant to sport.

The first continuum shown in the figure, from least functional to most functional, is of knee-dominant lower-body exercises. The least functional exercise I could imagine is a lying leg press. In the leg press, the athlete is lying on his or her back, and all stabilization is provided by the machine. The second example is a machine squat. The athlete has progressed up the functional continuum to a standing position—an improvement, but not a large one. Stability is still provided by the machine. The third example is a barbell squat. At this point the athlete is standing and self-stabilizing but is still two steps from the highest level of function. The next step in the progression is to work on one leg: a one-leg squat. At this point the exercise is extremely functional. The muscles of the lower body and trunk are now engaged as they would be in running or jumping. The final example is a one-leg squat while standing on an Airex pad. Now the athlete must engage the prime movers and stabilizers while getting additional balance training from the instability of the pad.

Least functional ⟶ Most functional

Lower-body exercises

Knee-dominant					
Type of exercise	Leg press	Machine squat	Barbell squat	One-leg squat	One-leg squat on Airex pad
Rationale	Lying, no stabilization by athlete	Standing, no stabilization by athlete	Two legs	One leg	One leg with additional challenge to balance

Hip-dominant					
Type of exercise	Leg curl	Back extension	Two-leg SLDL or RDL*	One-leg SLDL*	One-leg SLDL* on Airex pad
Rationale	Prone, non-functional action	Prone, functional action	Standing on two legs	Standing on one leg	Standing on one leg with additional challenge to balance

Upper-body exercises

Horizontal press					
Type of exercise	Machine bench press	Bench press	Dumbbell bench press	Push-up	Stability-ball push-up
Rationale	Supine, no stabilization by athlete	Supine, moderate stabilization	Supine, single-arm stabilization	Prone with closed chain	Prone with additional challenge to balance

Vertical press					
Type of exercise	Lat pull-down				Pull-up/chin-up

Horizontal pull					
Type of exercise	Machine row	Dumbbell row	Inverted row	One-arm, one-leg row	One-arm, two-leg rotational row

Torso exercises					
Type of exercise	Crunch	Russian twist	Standing lift	Standing rope lift	Machine-ball twist pass
Rationale	Lying, no rotation	Lying, with rotation	Standing without movement	Standing with weight stack	Standing with fast movement

* SLDL = Straight-leg deadlift; RDL = Romanian deadlift (modified straight-leg deadlift)

Figure 4.7 The functional continuum.

Functional Training and Female Athletes

Trainers and coaches are always curious how training should differ between male and female athletes. Often coaches pose questions that begin or end with "but I coach women." Female athletes are physically not very different from their male counterparts. At no point should coaches lower their expectations for female athletes. Most of what I have been told about training female athletes is untrue. Whether this is unintentional is not clear to me, but most of my preconceptions about training female athletes were not accurate.

The old theory that female athletes need to stay away from body-weight upper-body exercises is untrue. Female athletes are often held back by low expectations and preconceptions. Women and girls may not be able to begin with body-weight exercise, but they are able to progress to it. After training elite female athletes in basketball, soccer, field hockey, ice hockey, and figure skating, we have found that they are able to perform exercises such as dips, push-ups, and chin-ups when they progress properly. Although they may not possess the same upper-body strength as elite male athletes, they can develop excellent upper-body strength.

I have also found that female athletes are no more flexible than male athletes in similar sports. Our elite women's ice hockey players suffer from the same tightness in the hips that our men do. Our elite female soccer players are not significantly more flexible than their male counterparts. Athletes develop tightness and inflexibility based on the repetitive patterns of their sports, not on sex.

What I have found is that women are infinitely more coachable and not as extrinsically competitive as men. By extrinsically competitive, I mean that women are not nearly as worried about what another athlete is lifting. Women tend to focus more on what they can do and less on what others are doing. This makes them easier to coach.

I have also found that body image is a huge issue for female athletes. Female athletes are much more concerned about not building muscle than male athletes are. This is a unique societal influence that coaches must be aware of and work to overcome. Statistics about weight and body fat percentages are often fabricated, inflated, or deflated and provide unrealistic expectations for female athletes. The only body fat information athletes should be provided with should come from the coach, sports medicine staff, or exercise science department. Comparing the body composition of athletes at other schools or in other programs done with different methods, at different times, by different people is comparing apples and oranges. Female athletes must be reminded what height and weight is normal for their sport and their body type. Some athletic programs have adopted a head-in-the-sand approach to issues of eating disorders, body image, and nutrition by prohibiting coaches from weighing or measuring their female athletes. This does a great disservice to the female athletes. The solution is addressing the issues, not avoiding them. Education and the promotion of positive role models are essential for female athletes. Female athletes need to be exposed to photos of athletes similar to themselves that have a body composition that is considered acceptable. All too often visual role models for women are fashion models or entertainers that do not have the attributes of the average female athlete.

The major differences for training women and girls actually centers around equipment needs and progression. Most personal trainers and strength coaches do not consider the unique equipment needs of female athletes.

Equipment Needs for Training Female Athletes

All the following recommendations apply to training young athletes of either sex.

15-, 25-, and 35-pound Olympic bars—Many young and female athletes have little or no strength training background and may need lighter bars to begin with. Buy Olympic bars that take Olympic plates. Many companies now stock these new bars. Don't use conventional bars and one-inch-hole plates. Younger athletes should look like everyone else in the weight room.

Dumbbells in 2.5-pound increments—Custom-manufactured dumbbells in 2.5-pound increments are ideal. Five-pound increments do not allow younger or less-trained athletes to progress at reasonable rates. Consider that when less-experienced athletes advance from two 15-pound dumbbells to two 20-pound dumbbells, they are progressing from 30 pounds to 40 pounds, an increase of 33 percent. Would you ask a stronger athlete to go from 60-pound dumbbells to 80-pound dumbbells in one week?

1.25-pound PlateMates®—If you have only five-pound-increment dumbbells, Plate-Mates are the solution. PlateMates are simply 1.25-pound magnets that allow you to increase a dumbbell's weight by 2.5 pounds (one PlateMate on each side). Make sure to purchase the proper PlateMates for your style of dumbbell: hexagonal or round. Round PlateMates do not work well on hexagonal dumbbells and could pose a safety hazard.

1.25-pound Olympic plates—1.25-pound Olympic plates are not common but can be purchased. The same logic described earlier applies. Moving from 45 pounds to 50 pounds is only a 5-pound jump, but it is also a 10 percent jump. Many female athletes will not be able to make this type of progression. The male example again illustrates this point. Ask a male athlete to jump from 300 to 330 on the bench press in one week. This is only a 10 percent jump, but would be impossible for any athlete.

Dip belts—As your athletes gain strength, they can start to perform weighted chin-ups and possibly weighted dips. Conventional dip belts can fall off small female athletes. Belts need to be custom made to fit a female athlete's waist.

Weight belt—Again most weight rooms are outfitted with weight belts. If you are a proponent of weight belts, make sure that you purchase some size 24 to 28 belts for the females. This is one clear area of difference. Females generally have smaller waists than males.

Once your facility is properly equipped, functional training for female athletes does not present any problems. With proper equipment, all the functional training concepts discussed in this book can be used by female athletes.

With the proper equipment, training programs for female athletes have most of the characteristics of programs for male athletes. One possible exception is the use of body weight as the initial resistance for upper-body exercise. Exercises such as push-ups and pull-ups may need to be modified for beginning female athletes. Although I believe that women and girls can develop excellent upper-body strength, they may not have it to begin with. In this case, they can do bench presses or similar exercises using a proper load instead of push-ups, and they can do chin-ups with bands or a machine such as the Gravitron®.

When you design a program, it is important to note that the most functional exercise is often not the most appropriate. Instead, you should follow the progressions outlined in this book, master the basics, and strive to develop great functional strength by the end of the program. These are the key points:

- Learn the basics.
- Use body weight first.
- Progress from simple to complex.

I have a simple rule: Everything has to look good. Exercises should look smooth and athletic. If athletes are struggling to master an exercise, they should go back a level and work toward mastery. Technique comes before all else, always before the amount of weight lifted.

5

LINEAR AND LATERAL WARM-UP

The obvious place to begin discussing the actual nuts and bolts of functional training is with the functional warm-up. Even the concept of warming up has changed with the advent of functional training. Coaches and trainers have often confused the concepts of flexibility development and warm-up. Although flexibility is important for long-term injury prevention, static flexibility work is not a critical or necessary part of warming up and may be counterproductive. Think about warming up from a commonsense perspective. Ask yourself a few simple questions:

- Can I prepare to move by standing still for extended periods of time?
- Should I move slowly, or not at all, to prepare myself to move quickly?
- Should I sit down and be still to prepare to be on my feet and moving?

Only if you answered yes to all the preceding questions would static stretching make sense during the warm-up. If you took rubber bands out of the freezer and prepared to use them by stretching them, what do you think would happen? You would easily break quite a few. This is why athletes frequently pull muscles.

Does this sound like heresy? Most new ideas usually do. Just remember, at one time we were sure that the world was flat. Although we have not done a formal study, our facilities train more athletes per day than any other that we know. We have 600 athletes training four times per week for 11 weeks each summer. This amounts to 26,400 workouts. None of our athletes, from pros down to middle school students, stretch prior to these workouts. In 2002, we did not have a single serious muscle pull that required medical treatment.

Our athletes do not do static stretches, but our warm-ups take 15 to 20 minutes and often leave an athlete exhausted. The warm-up should gradually increase the stress on the muscle. A proper warm-up progressively increases the intensity of the movement, up to full speed.

A secondary benefit of a functional warm-up is that it reinforces the fundamentals of speed development or lateral movement while also preparing the body to perform more intense speed improvement drills or lateral movement drills. The warm-up should emphasize proper foot placement in all drills so that while warming up, the athlete also begins to understand the relationship of foot position to force production. In simplest terms, feet put down under the hip can become accelerators. Feet put down in front of the body act as brakes. In addition, all drills should be done with perfect body position. Athletes should learn to move from the hips and not to bend at the waist.

Warm-up and movement training can be divided into linear days and lateral days. This division, which is the brainchild of Mark Verstegen of Athletes' Performance Institute in Tempe, Arizona, is the best way to logically organize the movement portions of the workout. Linear warm-up is used to prepare the athlete for forward- and backward-moving speed, plyometrics, and conditioning, and lateral warm-up is used to prepare the athlete for side-to-side movement, plyometrics, and conditioning.

Linear Active Warm-Up

The linear active warm-up is simply a grouping of sprint-related drills that begin to prepare the body for straight-ahead sprinting. Linear warm-up involves what most coaches would classify as form running. Form-running drills are actually a variation of a track-and-field dynamic warm-up. Not only are these drills great for teaching movement, but they are great for preparing the lower body for the speed work to follow.

Form-running drills allow an athlete to warm up one muscle area (the prime mover) while providing a gentle dynamic stretch to the antagonist. This is what makes the linear warm-up so beneficial. Both requirements of a proper warm-up are met in the linear warm-up: The muscle temperature is raised, and the muscle is actively taken through its full range of motion. Never assume that one of these two is enough. Stretching takes the muscle through its full range, but not actively. Jogging increases muscle temperature but does not take the muscle through anything resembling full range. To properly prepare athletes for most sports, a linear warm-up must include drills that are done both forward and in reverse, so it must also include backward running drills. Remember, going in reverse may not matter in track and field, but it will matter in most other sports. One of the major mistakes made in teaching speed is too much reliance on information from track and field. Although most of what we know about speed comes from track and field, you need to "think outside the box" to apply some of these concepts to other sports.

The linear active warm-up (table 5.1) focuses primarily on the three muscle groups most often strained in running activities: the hip flexors, hamstrings, and quadriceps. By the end of a proper linear warm-up, these muscle groups should have been taken through their full range of motion at a number of different speeds. This type of warm-up should precede sessions involving any type of linear movement such as sprints, plyometrics, track work, or shuttle runs. Never assume that raising muscle temperature is enough. The warm-up needs to prepare the muscle to move at the speed at which it will be required to move and to move through the range of motion required.

table 5.1

LINEAR ACTIVE WARM-UP (20 YARDS EACH)

High knee walk
High knee skip
High knee run
Heel-ups
Straight-leg skip
Straight-leg deadlift walk
Backward run
Backpedal
Backward lunge walk (begin in week 2)
Forward lunge walk (begin in week 3)
Inchworm

High Knee Walk

The high knee walk is a gentle start to the warm-up that begins to stretch the muscles of the posterior hip, most importantly the glutes. As you step forward, grasp the shin of the opposite leg and pull the knee toward the chest (see figure 5.1). Concentrate on extending the stepping leg, and get up on the toes. The action of extending the leg and rising on the toes wakes up the opposite hip flexor.

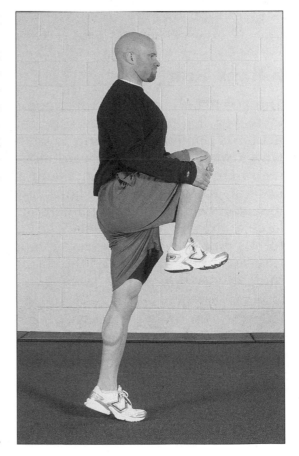

Figure 5.1 High knee walk.

High Knee Skip

The high knee skip (figure 5.2) is gentle skipping designed to put the hip flexor musculature into action. There is no emphasis on height or speed, only on rhythmic action.

Figure 5.2 High knee skip.

High Knee Run

The stress on the hip flexor group is increased in the high knee run. This action is similar to running in place with a small degree of forward movement. Emphasis is on maintaining an upright posture (weak athletes tend to lean forward or back) and getting a large number of foot contacts. The key to this drill is to maintain perfect posture so that the stress is on the correct muscles (see figure 5.3).

Figure 5.3 High knee run.

Heel-Ups

The heel-up, or butt kick as it is sometimes called, shifts the emphasis from the hip flexor to the hamstring. Actively bringing the heel to the butt serves not only to warm up the hamstring but also to take the quadriceps through its full range of motion (see figure 5.4).

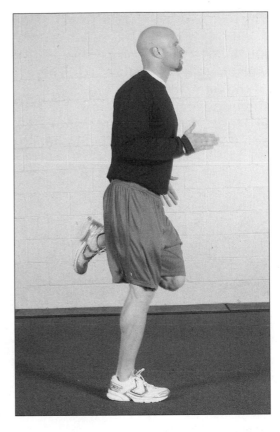

Figure 5.4 Heel-ups.

Straight-Leg Skip

The straight-leg skip (figure 5.5) increases the dynamic stretch on the hamstring while also activating the hip flexor. The hip flexor must contract powerfully to flex the hip with the leg straight. In addition, the dynamic stretch to the hamstring is increased by the straight-leg skipping action. The hands are held at shoulder height as a landmark for the height of the foot.

Figure 5.5 Straight-leg skip.

Straight-Leg Deadlift Walk

The straight-leg deadlift walk is another great active hamstring stretch. In addition, it offers excellent proprioceptive stimulus for the muscles in the ankle. Reach both arms out to the side while attempting to lift one leg up to waist height (see figure 5.6). This action provides an excellent dynamic stretch of the hamstring of the supporting leg while also activating the hamstring of the opposite leg as a hip extensor. To move forward, simply swing the back leg through for one large step. Be careful with this exercise, as it can cause some hamstring soreness in beginners.

Figure 5.6 Straight-leg deadlift walk.

Backward Run

It is important to clearly distinguish the backward run and the backpedal (described next). They may appear similar, but they have completely different purposes in the warm-up sequence. The backward run (figure 5.7) is literally running in reverse. The emphasis is on actively pushing with the front leg while reaching out aggressively with the back leg. Backward running strongly activates the hamstring as a hip extensor and dynamically stretches the anterior hip. This movement activates the hamstrings while stretching the hip flexors. In effect, it is the opposite of the straight-leg skip.

Figure 5.7 Backward run.

Backpedal

The backpedal is another backward movement, but it is used to warm up the quadriceps, not the hamstring. In the backpedal, the hips are kept low, and the feet are either under the body or in front of it (see figure 5.8). The action is a quadriceps-dominant push with no reach to the rear. The feet never get behind the body as they do in the backward run. Concentrate on the pushing leg extension action. This is a motion that football defensive backs perform easily but that many other athletes struggle with.

Figure 5.8 Backpedal.

Backward and Forward Lunge Walks

The backward and forward lunge walks are exercises that stretch out the anterior hip while warming up all of the leg and hip extensors. The backward or forward lunge walk is one of the best dynamic warm-up drills but should not be included in the warm-up until athletes have done a week of single-leg strength work. Begin the backward lunge walk in week 2, and add the forward lunge walk in week 3.

Lunge walks place more stress on the legs than many athletes are used to, and two 20-yard lunge walks can leave beginners so sore that they are unable to complete the rest of the workout. One area that the lunge walk stresses are the long adductors. Athletes who

Figure 5.9 Backward lunge walk.

have not performed lunge walks may cover 20 yards and then describe a feeling like a pulled groin muscle. Actually, this single-leg strength workout has stressed the long adductors in their function as hip extensors. This results in an unusual and unfamiliar soreness for many athletes. Generally, athletes at our training facility begin with the backward lunge walk (figure 5.9), as this stresses the knee extensors to a greater degree and places less stress on the long adductors.

Inchworm

The inchworm is one of the best total-body warm-up activities available and also one of the least popular. The inchworm is hard and leaves athletes tired. Begin in a push-up position. From the push-up position, drop the hips to stretch the abdominal area and then walk the feet up as close to the hands as possible while keeping the legs straight (see figure 5.10). This is done with small steps and no knee bend. This portion of the movement provides an excellent hamstring stretch. From this position, "walk" forward with the hands without moving the feet, finishing again with the hips down to stretch the abdominals. This "hand walk" portion provides an excellent upper-body warm-up, particularly for the scapulothoracic (shoulder blade) area. This sequence is continued over the target distance, which initially is 20 yards.

Figure 5.10 Inchworm.

Alternative Linear Warm-Up: Emphasis on Flexibility

The alternative linear warm-up (table 5.2) is an active warm-up that places more emphasis on dynamic flexibility and less on dynamic movement. The exercises used are closer to static stretching than those in the previously described linear warm-up. As a result, the distance covered in this warm-up is cut in half. All of the drills in this linear warm-up are done at a walking pace over 10 yards. Each drill is done once.

table 5.2

**ALTERNATIVE LINEAR WARM-UP:
FLEXIBILITY EMPHASIS (10 YARDS EACH)**

High knee walk with external rotation
Heel-up with internal rotation
Walking heel-up
Walking heel-up with SLDL*
Overhead lunge walk
Backward lunge walk with twist
SLDL walk forward
SLDL walk backward
Straight-leg crossover
Backward inchworm

* SLDL = straight-leg deadlift.

High Knee Walk With External Rotation

In the high knee walk with external rotation, grasp the shin (instead of the knee) with a double overhand grip and pull the shin to waist height (see figure 5.11). This causes the hip to externally rotate. At the same time, extend the hip of the supporting leg while rising up on the toes.

Figure 5.11 High knee walk with external rotation.

Heel-Up With Internal Rotation

The heel-up with internal rotation (figure 5.12) is also designed to stretch the hip, but into internal rotation. Grasp the foot with the palm of the hand on the inside of the arch. The hand must be supinated to get into this position. From this position, internally rotate (turn the foot out, thereby turning the leg internally) to stretch the hip external rotators. This is not simple, and some athletes who lack dynamic flexibility struggle with this movement.

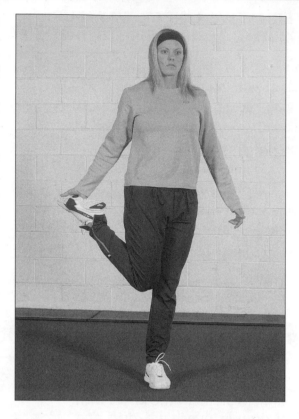

Figure 5.12 Heel-up with internal rotation.

Walking Heel-Up

Grasp the foot with the same-side hand and pull the heel to the butt with each step while walking (see figure 5.13). The grasping can instead be done with the opposite hand to increase the trunk involvement.

Figure 5.13 Walking heel-up.

Walking Heel-Up With Straight-Leg Deadlift

As in the previous exercise, pull the heel to the butt. In addition, lean forward, keeping the trunk straight, and lift the knee as high as possible (see figure 5.14). This exercise stresses the quadriceps and the rectus femoris of the lifted leg while also providing great proprioceptive input to the supporting foot and ankle.

Figure 5.14 Walking heel-up with straight-leg deadlift.

Overhead Lunge Walk

The overhead lunge walk is the same as the backward or forward lunge walk described in the first linear active warm-up, except the arms are held overhead to involve the upper body (figure 5.15). Grasp the thumb of the opposite hand, extend the elbows, and elevate the scapula.

Figure 5.15 Overhead lunge walk.

Backward Lunge Walk With Twist

Add a twisting action to the backward lunge walk: The opposite elbow is brought out over the front knee (figure 5.16). This action of lunging with trunk rotation increases the dynamic range of motion of the psoas (hip flexor muscles).

Figure 5.16 Backward lunge walk with twist.

Straight-Leg Deadlift Walk

The straight-leg deadlift walk forward is described earlier in the section on the linear active warm-up. This exercise is done forward and backward in both warm-ups because it provides excellent hamstring stretch and activation.

Straight-Leg Crossover

The straight-leg crossover is used to stretch both the hamstrings and the iliotibial (IT) band (a band of connective tissue that extends from the hip, along the side of the thigh, over the knee, to the top of the shinbone). Move to the left by crossing the right leg over the left, shift the left hip out to the left, and reach down and to the right toward the toes (see figure 5.17). The shifting of the hips in the direction of movement should be emphasized because it is key to stretching the IT band.

Figure 5.17 Straight-leg crossover.

Backward Inchworm

The backward inchworm is similar to the inchworm described in the section on the linear active warm-up (see page 36), but in reverse. The feet move away from the hands as you back down over a 10-yard distance. Begin in the push-up position and walk the hands and then the feet backward.

A linear warm-up should precede any linear speed or linear plyometric session. The intention is to have the warm-up be specific to the movements to follow. In a linear warm-up, the primary emphasis is on the hip flexors, quads, and hamstrings, as these are the muscles most frequently injured in linear speed work.

Developing Linear Speed Safely and Easily

Little can be said about linear speed that has not already been said by respected coaches in their videos and lectures over the past 10 years. Information on the technical aspects of speed is readily available from a number of different sources. Coaches are increasingly aware that athletes need to train for strength and power to improve speed. Many coaches use resisted and assisted methods of speed development. In addition, many companies provide coaches with commercial tools for speed development. Most of the advances in the past few years have been made in the area of lateral speed. We now have better brands and better tools.

I propose a system of speed development, or more aptly acceleration development, with an emphasis on injury prevention for team sports and large or small groups. This system of linear speed improvement is simple and easy to implement. The majority of speed work in this system is done over less than 10 yards and is actually acceleration work. Acceleration is of much greater importance in team sports than speed; however, coaches often use the words interchangeably. Coaches often express a desire for greater speed, when, in fact, most sports favor athletes with greater acceleration, not necessarily the fastest athletes. The simplest analogy to describe the difference between speed and acceleration is to look at automobiles. Every car can go 60 miles per hour. What separates a Porsche from a Yugo is how fast it can get from 0 to 60. An unnecessary concern with speed rather than acceleration is the pitfall of many treadmill-oriented speed development programs and many track-and-field-based programs.

The big questions in designing a speed development program involve which drills to perform, how far to perform them, and how often to perform them. The proposed system was initially field-tested with 400 athletes in the summer of 2000 in approximately 19,000 workouts (400 athletes working out 4 days per week for 12 weeks) and yielded fewer than 10 groin and hamstring strains.

The keys to the system are as follows:

■ Every speed workout is preceded by at least 15 minutes of dynamic warm-up and agility work. No static stretching is done before the workout.

■ Plyometrics are done after warm-up and before sprinting. This seems to provide a good speed-of-contraction bridge to sprinting.

The program is broken down into three 3-week phases that are based on simple concepts.

Weeks 1–3: Noncompetitive Speed

In the noncompetitive speed phase, simple drills work on the first three to five steps. Emphasis is on starting technique and first-step quickness. Athletes execute three to five hard pushes and then coast. Athletes initially are encouraged to run at slightly less than full speed to facilitate gradual muscular adaptation to sprinting. At no time should athletes race or compete in any form in this noncompetitive phase. The primary drills used in this phase are the lean, fall, and run (figure 5.18a) and the 90-degree lean, fall, and run (figure 5.18b) from Vern Gambetta's *Straight Ahead Speed* video (Gambetta Sports Systems, 1995). Generally only six 10-yard sprints are done each day.

a   *b*

Figure 5.18 (*a*) Lean, fall, and run drill. (*b*) Ninety-degree lean, fall, and run drill.

Weeks 4–6: Short Competitive Speed

In the second phase, a series of competitive drills are introduced, but the distance is limited. The intensity of the sprint work increases while the distance (volume) is maintained or even decreased. One of the difficulties of speed development programs is that coaches often cannot control or discern whether athletes are actually attempting to reach top speed during speed development sessions. The introduction of a competitive incentive ensures that athletes attempt to accelerate. The competitive incentive is simply a tennis ball. The short competitive speed phase consists of ball-drop sprints from various double- and single-leg start positions (see figure 5.19). Ball-drop sprints ensure that athletes accelerate for a short burst of speed. Even gifted athletes do not generally exceed five to seven yards when a tennis ball is dropped from shoulder height. Do not underestimate the competitive nature of athletes. Athletes frequently lay out to get the ball in ball-drop sprints, although this is discouraged. Ball-drop sprints create a competitive environment that encourages acceleration without excessively stressing the hamstrings or hip flexors.

Figure 5.19 Ball-drop sprint.

Weeks 7–9: Long Competitive Speed

In the third phase athletes sprint against a partner from many different start positions. Chase sprints and breakaway belt sprints are done from standing and lying starting positions. At this point, sprint workouts become tag games, with athletes alternating as the chaser or the chased. Athletes' accelerative abilities are challenged in a competitive atmosphere that guarantees maximum effort. In this phase, athletes are limited to a 10- to 20-yard tag zone.

The speed development program outlined yields excellent results when combined with a proper warm-up, a proper lower-body strength program, and a progressive plyometric program. Athletes progress gradually from individually paced starting and first-step drills to highly competitive tag races over a nine-week period to ensure proper muscular adaptation. Either volume or intensity is increased in each phase, but never both. In the lower-body strength program, exercises are performed twice weekly for both knee extension (front squat and single-leg variations) and hip extension (straight-leg and bent-leg variations that emphasize glutes and hamstrings). The combination of progressive speed, progressive plyometrics, and progressive strength training has resulted in an injury rate of less than 1 per 1,000 workouts at our training facility.

Lateral Warm-Up: Improving Lateral Agility and Speed

The lateral warm-up prepares the body for workouts devoted to improving lateral movement. The lateral warm-up consists of eight minutes of agility ladder work followed by five minutes of lateral dynamic flexibility. The key is to stress the abductor and adductor groups to a greater degree than is possible in the linear warm-up. The warm-up should be specific to the demands of the activity. The lateral warm-up prepares the athlete for the lateral movement and lateral speed progressions to follow.

In addition to agility ladder drills, the athlete needs to stress the hip area with exercises like the lateral squat and stationary Spider-Man.

Lateral Squat

Most coaches recognize the lateral squat as a groin stretch. I prefer to view the lateral squat as a dynamic exercise to improve the hips' range of motion in the frontal plane. Begin with the feet four feet apart and sit to the right, keeping the left leg straight (figure 5.20). The weight is kept on the right heel as you attempt to sit as tall and as low as possible. Hold the bottom position for one second, and then switch to the left heel.

Figure 5.20 Lateral squat.

Stationary Spider-Man

In the stationary Spider-Man, assume a push-up position and step forward as if to try to step just outside of the right hand with the right foot (see figure 5.21). From this position, drop the right elbow to the ground. Then return the foot to its original position and switch sides. Hold this dynamic stretch no more than one second in the elongated position. This is not a static stretch in the warm-up, although it can be used as such after the workout.

Figure 5.21   Stationary Spider-Man.

Lateral Agility Progression

The old adage that you can't teach speed was disproved years ago. However, many coaches still believe that agility and coordination cannot be taught. In truth, change of direction, the essence of lateral movement, can be taught and comes down to three simple criteria.

1. Do you have the single-leg strength necessary not only to stop movement but to restart movement after a stop? Single-leg strength is the essential quality for developing agility. Without single-leg strength, no amount of agility will enable athletes to make cuts at top speed.
2. Can you decelerate? Eccentric strength is the real key to deceleration. Think of eccentric strength not as the ability to lower a weight but instead as the ability to bring the body to a rapid stop. Eccentric strength is the ability to put on the brakes.
3. Can you land with stability? Is the proprioceptive system prepared to create a stable landing?

Athletes need to understand the most basic concept of agility: To move to the left, you must push off with the right foot. You never get anywhere fast by stepping in the direction that you are going; you have to literally push yourself in the direction you want to go with the foot that is farthest away. However, before you can make the push necessary for change of direction, you need to decelerate and land with stability. Most of what passes as agility training is simply timing movement. A better philosophy is to *teach* movement, not *time* movement. Do not just ask athletes to run around cones in an attempt to lower their time. Teach athletes the proper way to execute a right turn, a left turn, or a 45-degree cut.

To do this, begin with a simple drill called one-two stick. The essence of this drill is the "stutter step." The stutter step is the basic component of most offensive evasive maneuvers in sport. The crossover dribble in basketball and the wide dribble in field or ice hockey are just a few examples of executing a stutter step to elude an opponent.

All the lateral movement drills are taught using flat plastic hoops to teach foot placement. I advise against running laterally over mini-hurdles, because lateral movement in sports is generally more of a shuffle action than a step-over action. The feet should move quickly, accurately, and low to the ground.

To clarify the progression, exercises are classified as level 1, 2, or 3. Level 1 exercises are the simplest exercises, used for beginners. Level 2 exercises are slightly more intense, and level 3 exercises are the most difficult. All athletes, regardless of training stage, should begin with level 1 exercises for the first three weeks of training. Attempting to progress too rapidly can lead to injury. Athletes should progress only when they have mastered an exercise.

One-Two Stick

 Level 1

The one-two stick teaches athletes to land stably with proper mechanics and to push with the left to move to the right. Begin standing on the left foot in the first hoop. The action is a simple right-left-right series of steps. Push off with the left foot, step over hoop 2 into hoop 3 with the right foot, step into hoop 2 with the left foot, and finish on the right foot with a stable, single-leg landing in hoop 4 (see figure 5.22). Then repeat the action to the opposite side,

Figure 5.22 One-two stick.

left-right-left. Land on the inside ball of the foot with the knee more inward than the foot. With this type of landing, you can immediately move back in the opposite direction. In addition, keeping your weight on the inside ball of the foot when changing direction makes it nearly impossible to sprain an ankle.

One-Two Cut

 Level 2 The one-two cut is the second step in the progression for learning change of direction. This purely lateral drill is exactly the same as the one-two stick, except without the stable landing. Move side to side through the hoops as rapidly as proper mechanics allow. The emphasis is again on proper footwork, keeping the weight on the inside ball of the foot, and keeping the knee inward of the ankle.

Assisted One-Two Cut

 Level 3 The third step of the progression is the assisted one-two cut. A surgical tubing belt is used to assist the athlete in the return phase of the drill and to provide resistance to the initial push-off. The drill is the same as the one-two cut, but the athlete is pulled back by the surgical tubing, requiring the athlete to produce even greater eccentric decelerative force (see figure 5.23).

Figure 5.23 Assisted one-two cut.

Forty-Five-Degree One-Two Cut

Level 4 In the fourth level of the lateral agility progression the footwork is the same as in previous one-two cut drills, but a linear component is added. Execute the stutter step at a 45-degree angle, using the same right-left-right, left-right-left action as you move forward with the hips and shoulders square (see figure 5.24).

Figure 5.24 Forty-five-degree one-two cut.

Lateral Speed Progression

The previous progression teaches change of direction, while the drills that follow initially train pure lateral speed and then combine lateral speed with change of direction. As in the lateral agility drills, flat hoops are used instead of hurdles to facilitate proper footwork. Strive for fast feet low to the ground, not high-knee action done over small hurdles.

Lateral Hoop Run and Stick: Three Hoops

Level 1 In the lateral run and stick, move laterally, touching both feet down in turn in the hoops. Run sideways, placing one foot then the other in the hoop. No hoops are skipped with either foot. If you are moving from right to left, a right foot push initiates the movement and is followed by a left-to-right action in each of the three hoops (see figure 5.25). The drill concludes with a stable landing on the left foot outside the third ring. The drill is then repeated to the opposite side.

Figure 5.25 Lateral hoop run and stick.

Lateral Hoop Run and Stick: Five Hoops

Level 2 In level 2 of the progression, the drill is the same, but the number of hoops is increased to five. This allows athletes to pick up more speed and consequently to decelerate greater forces.

Lateral Hoop Run and Stick: Seven Hoops

Level 3 In level 3, the drill is the same, but two additional hoops are added.

Lateral Hoop Run with Return: Two Hoops

 Level 4 In level 4, the benefits of the one-two cut and the lateral hoop run are combined in one drill for both lateral speed and change of direction. In the lateral hoop run with return, athletes move through two hoops, decelerate, and then move back in the opposite direction (figure 5.26). This drill can be progressed by adding hoops one at a time.

Figure 5.26 Lateral hoop run with return.

These progressions might seem too simple, too mechanical, or too perfunctory. But I strongly believe that most athletes need to be taught concepts that appear to be innate in great athletes. Coaches should not assume that athletes know how best to move from place to place but should teach this. Training for agility should involve *teaching* movement, not *timing* movement.

The Role of Static Stretching: Postworkout Flexibility

Because the warm-up and speed development drills did not include static stretching, you may have come to the conclusion that flexibility is not important. This could not be further from the truth. Flexibility is critical, but stretching must be done at the appropriate time and with the proper purpose. The warm-up should be dynamic and prepare the athlete to perform the day's activities. Flexibility work, on the other hand, is most often done after the workout to restore tissue length and to prevent long-term overuse injury. Athletes do not pull muscles because they lack flexibility; they pull muscles because they are unprepared in either the short term or the long term. Do not think of flexibility as a part of warm-up but rather as a part of your long-term injury prevention strategy. For a full discussion of flexibility, see the National Academy of Sports Medicine (www.NASM.org) course on integrated flexibility training.

This chapter provides some simple yet effective progressions to improve both linear and lateral speed. The athlete moves from a specific warm-up to drills that are appropriate for the movement emphasis of the day. Specific days are devoted to linear speed, and others are devoted to lateral speed. This simple system allows coaches to design workouts easily and athletes to be properly prepared for the stresses to follow. Static flexibility work is deliberately saved for the end of the workout. The warm-ups incorporate progressions for the neuromuscular system and are based on current science on warm-ups and injury reduction to ensure a safe approach. Remember, functional training is training that makes sense. A warm-up that relates to the drills to be done makes sense. Warming up by moving makes sense.

LOWER-BODY STRENGTH AND BALANCE PROGRESSIONS

The development of functional lower-body strength should be the primary area of emphasis in any high-quality training program. Lower-body strength training should generally begin with body-weight squats. Simply teaching an athlete the body-weight squat reveals important information about strength, flexibility, and injury potential. Body-weight squats can be used to assess flexibility in the hips, ankles, and hamstrings and the general strength of the lower body.

Athletes who cannot body-weight squat to a position with the thighs parallel to the floor (figure 6.1a) are deficient in either ankle, hip, or hamstring flexibility. The athlete should be enabled to squat to the proper depth by raising the heels on a one-by-four board or a specially made wedge. This does not harm the knees in any way. The idea that elevating the heels increases the stress on the knees is not supported by any scientific research. Athletes who have difficulty keeping the knees from moving past the toes are also deficient in either flexibility or strength.

An explanation of the importance of knee-dominant squatting versus ankle-dominant squatting is necessary. When most athletes hear the directive "squat," their minds tell their bodies to lower their hips the easiest way possible. For weaker athletes the easiest way is often one that does not stress the weak muscles (usually the quadriceps). Weaker athletes or athletes returning from injury often attempt to lower the center of gravity by initially driving the knees forward out over the toes until the limit of the ankle range of motion is reached (figure 6.1b). Then and only then does the movement begin to center on the knee joint. This type of ankle-dominant squatting leads to excessive knee flexion in order to reach a position with the thighs parallel to the ground. This is the squatter's paradox. Most therapists and athletic trainers describe squatting based on knee angle. Patients are directed to squat to a 90-degree knee angle. A knee angle of 90 degrees can be reached far before a parallel squat is

Figure 6.1 *(a)* Proper and *(b)* improper squatting technique.

reached. Strength coaches do not define squat depth by knee angle but rather by a parallel relationship of the femur (thighbone) to the floor, which often results in a knee angle greater than 135 degrees if the athlete is an ankle-dominant squatter. This type of ankle-dominant squatting is frequently seen in athletes with knee pain or patellar tendinitis (tendinitis in the quadriceps tendon).

The key to the squat is to combine the therapist's desire to limit the athlete's knee range of motion with the coach's desire to get the athlete's thigh parallel to the floor. Coaches, trainers, and therapists need to speak the same language. The athlete must be given instructions that address both the coach's and the trainer or therapist's concerns. The athlete must be taught to body-weight squat in a manner that minimizes range of motion at the ankle and maximizes range of motion at the knee. The athlete can then progress to the hands-free front squat.

The front squat is the foundation of the program. Although most conventional strength programs emphasize the back squat, my experience has shown me that the front squat provides excellent strength development with a decreased incidence of injury. Full squats are always used in this program. The full squat is defined as one in which the top of the thigh is parallel to the floor. Half squats or quarter squats should never be used. No one does half or quarter curls to save the elbows; the knees are no different. Partial squats cannot fully develop the glutes, hamstrings, and lower back. In addition, half squats and quarter squats present a larger risk of back injury due to the heavier weights used in partial movements. Athletes with normal flexibility can squat to a position with the thighs parallel to the floor with no heel elevation. Less flexible athletes can use heel elevation. Increased strength in squatting movements is the first step in developing speed and increasing vertical jump.

Developing a Safe Squatting Style

The following steps are critical for developing a technically correct and safe squatting style.

Step 1: Learning the Hands-Free Body-Weight Squat

For the hands-free body-weight squat (figure 6.2), start with the arms extended out in front of the body with the hands at shoulder height. This teaches athletes to eventually carry the bar on the shoulders, not on the wrists. Do not skip this step; it is critical. The chest should be up, and the upper and lower back should be arched and tight. Feet should be approximately shoulder-width apart and slightly turned out, approximately 10 to 15 degrees. The stance may be widened to obtain proper depth if flexibility is a problem. A one-by-four board, a 10-pound plate, or a specially made wedge may be placed under the heels if the athlete tends to lean forward during the descent, if the heels lose contact with the ground, or if the pelvis rotates posteriorly in the descent. Although many authorities caution against an object under the heels, athletes at our training facility have experienced great success and no knee pain with this method.

The Descent

1. Prior to descending into the squat, inhale deeply to fully inflate the lungs. The fully inflated lungs brace the upper and lower back.

2. When descending into the squat, concentrate on sitting back and placing the body weight on the heels. Placing the body weight on the midfoot or toes causes an undesirable forward lean. Do not let the breath out. Keep the hands level with the shoulders.

3. Descend slowly until the tops of the thighs are parallel to the floor. Partial squats build the ego but not the legs. Squat to the proper depth with light weights for better results.

4. In the descent, the knees should stay over the toes. Do not pinch the knees in; allow the knees to spread outward over the toes.

The Ascent

1. Concentrate on driving upward with the chest out, bringing the hips up and forward.

2. Drive the heels into the floor.

Figure 6.2 Hands-free body-weight squat.

3. Exhale slowly. Let the air slowly hiss out of the lungs as if you had punctured a tire.

Please remember that the squat is a safe movement when done properly. Start with body weight to develop proper technique and progress to higher weights only if technique is perfect. Injuries occur only when athletes fail to adhere to proper technique.

Step 2: Learning the Hands-Free Front Squat

Begin with the arms extended out in front of the body with the hands at shoulder height. A bar is placed across the front deltoids in contact with the throat. The hands deliberately do not touch the bar. This teaches athletes to carry the bar on the shoulders, not on the wrists, as shown in figure 6.3. Do not neglect this critical point. Follow the descent and ascent instructions for the hands-free body-weight squat.

Figure 6.3 Hands-free front squat.

Step 3: Learning the Clean-Grip Front Squat

Do not use a crossover grip in the clean-grip front squat (figure 6.4). Athletes must be able to execute a proper front squat to be able to clean properly. The front squat start position is used for the clean catch, the push jerk, and the push press.

Even if you elect to use the back squat as your primary lower-body exercise, the front squat is actually an excellent way to teach the squat. Why?

■ Front squats require perfect body position.

■ Front squats develop shoulder flexibility, a big plus in the bench press–dominated world of strength training. Flexibility is enhanced only if a clean grip is used, which I recommend.

■ Front squats require less weight and put less pressure on the ego. No one seems to beg for more weight in the front squat.

It is important to note that if you are having trouble with proper squat technique, you are attempting to use too much weight too soon or you have inadequate flexibility in the hips and Achilles tendons. The optimal way to stretch for the squat is to sit in the full squat position, place the elbows on the inner sides of the knees, and push the knees out over the toes while arching the back (figure 6.5). Master the technique over the first month if necessary, and work hard on the single-leg exercises after your squat workout.

Figure 6.4 Clean-grip front squat.

Figure 6.5 Squat stretch.

Canadian strength coach Charles Poliquin advocates using straps, as pictured in figure 6.6, to assist in developing the flexibility necessary to do a clean-grip front squat. This excellent alternative grip is the only alternative grip I recommend. The use of straps as shown can cause most complaints about the discomfort of the front squat to disappear. We have found that our athletes perform a one-repetition maximum (1RM) front squat at 80 to 90 percent of their back-squat 1RM after 12 weeks of training.

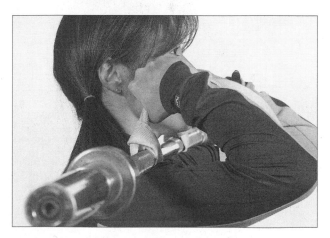

Figure 6.6 Using straps with the clean-grip front squat.

Adding Instability to the Front Squat

Over the past few years, my training philosophy has changed in regard to the number of times to perform a lift in a week. The old philosophy was a heavy–light system in which a specific lift, such as the front squat, was done twice per week, once with heavy weight and once with light. Light days were difficult to enforce and regulate. Instead of light days, I now opt for unstable days. Unstable days serve two purposes. Unstable-surface work forces the athlete to lift lighter while also developing balance and proprioception. The unstable surface also requires the athlete to concentrate on technique and weight distribution to be successful.

Balance-Board Squats

Balance-board squats (figure 6.7) are an excellent way to provide additional proprioceptive stress to the lower body while continuing to develop technique in the front squat. This drill is done exactly the same as the clean-grip front squat except that you stand on a balance board such as the Reebok Core Board. For heavy balance-board squats, our boards are constructed of three-quarter-inch plywood measuring 18 inches by 36 inches, attached to a base made from a four-by-four. These boards must be sturdy. The four-by-four is trimmed with a router to provide a surface of slightly less than three inches in contact with the floor. The base is attached to the four-by-four with both construction adhesive and screws. Please realize that if you construct your own balance boards, you assume responsibility for the construction quality.

Figure 6.7 Balance-board squat.

Developing Single-Leg Strength

Single-leg strength is a quality that has frequently been ignored in strength programs but is essential to the improvement of speed and balance and the prevention of injury. Single-leg strength is the essence of functional lower-body strength; a case can be made that all double-leg activities, such as squats, are nonfunctional for most sports. Although viewing double-leg squatting as nonfunctional may be extreme, it emphasizes the need for single-leg exercise in any strength program. Unfortunately, most strength programs focus on conventional double-leg exercises such as squats, leg presses, or unequivocally nonfunctional leg exercises such as leg extensions or leg curls. Ask yourself a simple question. How many sports are played with both feet in contact with the ground at the same time? The answer is not many. Most sport skills are performed on one leg. For this simple reason, it is critical that single-leg strength be a focal point of the strength program.

It is important to note that single-leg strength is specific and cannot be developed through double-leg exercises. The actions of the pelvic stabilizers are different in a single-leg stance than in a double-leg stance. Single-leg exercises force the gluteus medius (a muscle in the buttocks) and quadratus lumborum (a low-back muscle) to operate as stabilizers, which are critical in sport skills. In addition, single-leg strength is now recognized as a key in injury reduction and has become a staple of most reconditioning programs and knee injury prevention programs.

These exercises are classified as level 1, 2, or 3. Remember that all athletes, regardless of training stage, should begin with level 1 exercises for the first three weeks of training. Almost all level 2 exercises can be done with external load by more advanced athletes, but remember that athletes should progress only when they have mastered an exercise. After athletes have mastered a level 1 single-leg strength exercise, they can progress to a level 2 single-leg strength exercise or to the addition of an unstable surface to the level 1 exercise. Progression to an unstable surface should be as follows:

1. Half foam roller, round side up
2. Half foam roller, round side down
3. Airex pad

Most of the single-leg exercises initially use a body-weight progression. This simply means that the athlete uses body weight only (no external weight) for the first three weeks but increases reps each week from 8 to 10 to 12 per leg. This is a simple progressive resistance concept. More advanced athletes might want to begin with external loads (bar, dumbbells, or weight vest), but this is discouraged initially if the athletes do not have experience with single-leg training. As athletes become more advanced, any single-leg exercise can be added into the program as long as no fewer than five reps are used.

Split Squat

The split squat (figure 6.8) is a great simple exercise for developing single-leg strength. This exercise is always step 1 in our single-leg progression. Assume a long lunge position, which provides two solid, stable points on the ground. From this position, touch the back knee to the floor while keeping the front knee over the ankle.

Please note that this is not a lunge exercise. The exercise involves no foot movement. An added benefit of the split squat is the development of dynamic flexibility in the hip flexor muscles.

Technique Points

- Keep the front knee over the ankle and concentrate on dropping the back knee down to the floor.
- Keep the head and chest up. A position with the hands behind the head works best.
- Dumbbells or a bar can be added in the front-squat or back-squat position.
- Concentrate on lowering the hips while keeping the front knee over the ankle. The knee of the back leg should be slightly flexed. You should feel as if you are doing a slight hip flexor stretch when positioned correctly.

Figure 6.8 Split squat.

Overhead Split Squat

Level 1 The overhead split squat (figure 6.9) is an excellent variation of the split squat that develops flexibility in the hip area and shoulder complex simultaneously. In addition, the overhead split squat stimulates the muscles responsible for thoracic extension, thereby aiding postural improvement. This single body-weight exercise improves single-leg strength, lower-body flexibility, and upper-body flexibility. This "three for the price of one" exercise is a hugely beneficial movement.

The only difference from the split squat described previously is that a stick is held overhead with the elbows locked, just over the back of the head.

Figure 6.9 Overhead split squat.

One-Leg Bench Squat

 Level 2 For the one-leg bench squat (figure 6.10), get into a position similar to that for the split squat, except place the back foot on a bench. There is one stable point of support on the floor and one slightly less stable point on the bench. This is a slight increase in difficulty because the back leg can provide very little assistance. From this position, descend until the front thigh is parallel to the floor and the back knee is nearly touching the floor. Like the split squat, this exercise is done with no foot movement and improves the dynamic flexibility of the hip flexor muscles.

This exercise can be done as a body-weight exercise, following the 8-10-12 body-weight progression described earlier, or as a strength exercise with dumbbells or a bar for as few as five reps (e.g., three sets of five reps per leg).

Figure 6.10 One-leg bench squat

One-Leg Box Squat

 Level 3 The one-leg box squat (figure 6.11) is the king of single-leg exercises. It is the most difficult and most beneficial of all single-leg exercises. Follow the progression from split squat to one-leg bench squat before attempting the one-leg box squat. The one-leg box squat requires the use of one leg without any contribution to balance or stability from the opposite leg. The pelvic muscles must function as stabilizers without the benefit of the opposite leg's touching the ground or a bench. The importance of this point cannot be overstated, as pelvic muscle stabilization is needed in all sprinting actions. The stance leg must produce force without any assistance from the swing leg. Do not become discouraged if you are unable to perform this exercise

immediately. Most athletes feel unsteady or clumsy the first few times. One of the major benefits of single-leg squats is the balance that they develop. You might require a few sessions to even begin to become comfortable with the one-leg box squat.

Technique Points

- Stand on a box holding a pair of five-pound dumbbells and attempt to squat to a position with the thigh parallel with the floor. Although dumbbells may not seem like a good idea, they provide a counterbalance, and we have found that they make the movement easier to learn.
- Concentrate on keeping the weight on the heel to minimize movement at the ankle and to keep the knee from moving beyond the big toe in the bottom position. Standing on a plate or specially made wedge can be extremely helpful.
- As you begin to squat, raise the dumbbells to shoulder level to facilitate sitting back on the heel.
- It is critical to begin by bending at the knee and not by bending at the ankle. Watch carefully for this.

Most athletes should begin with three sets of five reps with five-pound dumbbells. You can progress by increasing reps or by increasing the weight of the dumbbells, depending on where you are in the training cycle (for example, whether you are in a strength or muscle hypertrophy phase). As with the one-leg bench squat, do no fewer than five reps per leg.

Figure 6.11 One-leg box squat.

Lunge

Level 3

The lunge (figure 6.12) is another great single-leg exercise and is mistakenly considered by many to be an easy alternative to the squat. In actuality, the lunge is a very productive addition to the program. The key benefit of the lunge, and the reason it is an advanced exercise, is that the leg muscles must cause deceleration as the body moves forward. The lunge is a level 3 exercise because the body must be properly prepared for the deceleration component. In addition, lunges are an excellent dynamic stretching movement for the hip area and should be included in strength training and warm-up routines for this reason alone. Athletes who have had groin or hip flexor problems will find the lunge a very beneficial exercise.

Technique Points

- The back should stay tight and arched, and the upper body should stay erect.
- The movement begins by standing with the feet together.
- The step should be approximately as long as the athlete is tall. The step should be long enough to stretch the hip flexor muscles of the rear leg.
- The movement ends by pushing back so the feet are back together.

Figure 6.12 Lunge.

As many as 15 reps on each leg can be done for endurance. Lunges can be included in leg circuits in combination with other exercises.

Additional Functional Single-Leg Variations

These functional single-leg variations add variety to any program but are especially intended for experienced athletes and rehabilitation programs. The previous single-leg strength exercises are the basic core exercises for beginners. Too much variation results in an athlete who is a jack of all trades and master of none. Keep to the basic progression until competence is established. When athletes have demonstrated a high level of competence, the following exercises can be used for variety.

Step-Up

Level 1

The step-up (figure 6.13) is an alternative to the squat for athletes with back or knee problems. Step-ups are a level 1 variation for athletes struggling with the split squat. Step-ups generally put less stress on both the knees and the low back than conventional squats. In addition, significantly less weight is needed in the step-up than in the squat. However, step-ups may cause more discomfort for athletes with knee problems than any of the previously mentioned single-leg exercises due to the lack of an initial eccentric contraction. The step-up is not a preferred single-leg movement because athletes can cheat too easily by pushing off with the foot on the ground.

Another excellent variation of the step-up is the high-box step-up. In this exercise a box places the hip parallel to the knee. A higher box increases the contribution of the hamstrings and glutes and minimizes the ability to cheat using the foot on the ground.

Figure 6.13 Step-up.

Technique Points

- Ninety percent of the foot should be on the box. A slight portion of the heel may be off the box.
- Push down through the heel and midfoot; avoid shifting the weight to the ball of the foot.
- Keep the head and chest up, and always lead up with the head and shoulders.
- In the top position, balance on the supporting foot. Do not let the opposite foot touch the box.

Lateral Step-Up

Level
1
The lateral step-up (figure 6.14) is a modification of the step-up that provides greater stress to the adductor muscles of the inner thigh. The exercise is similar to the forward step-up, except you begin to one side of the box and step up laterally. The lateral step-up can be used by athletes in any sport but is an excellent variation for soccer or hockey players.

The same technique points for the step-up apply to the lateral step-up. The finish position for the lateral step-up also requires balancing on one leg.

Figure 6.14 Lateral step-up.

Slide-Board Back Lunge

The slide-board back lunge is an excellent single-leg exercise that combines single-leg strength, dynamic flexibility, and moderate instability. This is a great movement for both training and rehabilitation. In order not to monopolize the slide boards, this exercise can be done on a four-foot length of slide-board top material rather than a slide board itself. Wear one slide-board shoe on the back foot, and slide the foot back in a back lunge (figure 6.15). The back foot slides forward and back while the front foot performs a single-leg squat. Place the hands behind the head, and keep the front knee over the midfoot.

Use a body-weight progression with this exercise because of the additional stretch and instability component.

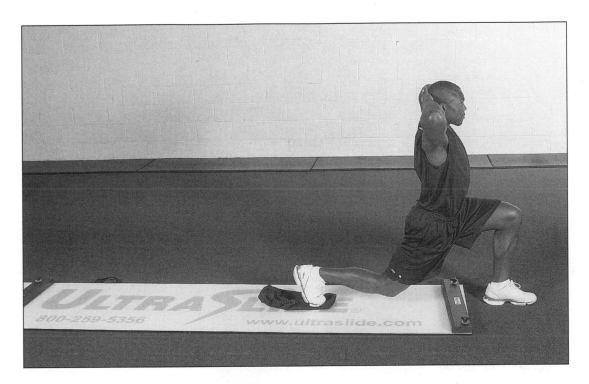

Figure 6.15 Slide-board back lunge.

Elevated Slide-Board Back Lunge

Level 3 This is nearly identical to the slide-board back lunge, but the front foot is elevated on a four- to six-inch step to provide additional range of motion (see figure 6.16). This is an excellent progression for athletes who have experienced hip flexor strains.

Figure 6.16 Elevated slide-board back lunge.

Skater's One-Leg Squat

Level 3 This is a hockey-specific version of the one-leg box squat. Instead of keeping the torso erect and placing the free leg out in front, the torso is brought down to touch the thigh (figure 6.17) and the free leg is extended off the back of the box. This forward flexed position simulates the skater's starting position.

Figure 6.17 Skater's one-leg squat.

Lateral Squat

Level 1 The lateral body-weight squat is used both in the lateral warm-up and as a strength exercise. The lateral squat is an excellent exercise to promote dynamic flexibility of the adductor musculature. Stand with the feet approximately four feet apart and sit to one side (figure 6.18). Keep the weight on the heel as you sit, and keep the knee over the toe. Wider is better in this exercise. Athletes taller than five feet eight inches will have difficulty performing this exercise with their feet less than four feet apart.

Use the body-weight progression for the lateral squat. In a departure from the basic philosophy of this program, a bar can be used in the back-squat position to add weight.

Figure 6.18 Lateral squat.

Developing Single-Leg Stability

Athletes often perform exercises such as the split squat and one-leg bench squat reasonably well but struggle with the one-leg box squat. Frequently these are athletes who suffer from knee problems such as chondromalacia patellae (softening of the knee cartilage), patellar tendinitis, or other patellofemoral syndromes. My experience has taught me that these athletes generally share a common difficulty in stabilizing the lower extremity while squatting due to a weak gluteus medius. The gluteus medius is an often-neglected muscle of the hip whose primary function is to stabilize the lower extremity in single-leg movements such as running, jumping, or squatting.

In many athletes this muscle is either too weak to perform its function or is not "turned on" neurologically. As a result, the support structures of the knee are forced to provide stability instead of the gluteus medius. This may mean pain in the iliotibial band (IT), in the patellar tendon, or under the kneecap. For many years these problems were blamed on poor quadriceps strength, and doctors and therapists prescribed simple, nonfunctional exercise like leg extensions to solve the problem. Recently therapists and athletic trainers have begun to recognize the role of the gluteus medius in these knee problems. Correction first involves isolation exercises to teach athletes how to use the gluteus medius and to promote simple strengthening. Two simple exercises, the bent-leg hip abduction and straight-leg hip abduction, are used for this purpose.

Bent-Leg Hip Abduction

To perform a bent-leg hip abduction (figure 6.19), lie on the side with the knees bent 90 degrees and the hips flexed to 45 degrees. The soles of the feet should be in line with spine. This position is like the hook-lying position (lying on the back with the feet flat on the floor and both the hips and knees flexed), only on the side. A 15- to 20-inch band is placed around both thighs to resist the side-lying abduction. Abduct (raise) the leg, keeping the feet together without rotating at the lumbar spine. The hips and shoulders should remain in line, one over the other, and all the motion should come from the hip. Generally, sets of 10 reps are done in week 1, and 2 reps per week are added. Most athletes erroneously make this a trunk rotation exercise. Athletes must abduct the thigh with no movement at the lumbar spine.

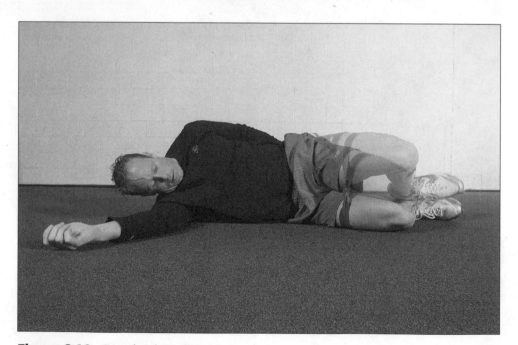

Figure 6.19 Bent-leg hip abduction.

Straight-Leg Hip Abduction

To do a straight-leg hip abduction (figure 6.20), lie on the side with both legs extended and the body in a straight line. The top leg is slightly hyperextended at the hip, and the femur is internally rotated. From this position, lift the leg to the side. These exercises are valuable in helping athletes learn to isolate and activate the gluteus medius.

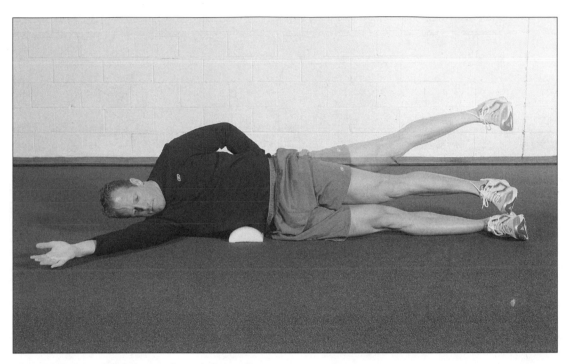

Figure 6.20 Straight-leg hip abduction.

This chapter describes the foundation of a proper lower-body strength program. Squatting and performing single-leg exercises are two keys for developing speed and power. Follow the progressions and guidelines given. Don't look for an easy way out by reverting to machine training for the lower body. An athlete cannot develop balance, flexibility, and strength while sitting or lying down. The difficult road is often the best road.

HIP EXTENSIONS AND HEALTHY HAMSTRINGS

The muscles that extend the hip, primarily the gluteus maximus and hamstring group, are often neglected, even in many functional training programs. Programs frequently place excessive emphasis on the knee extensors and neglect the hip extensors. Even more disturbing, the muscles that extend the hip, especially the hamstrings, are often mistakenly trained as knee flexors. In nonfunctional strength programs, many muscle groups are still trained according to outdated understandings of their function. Although some anatomy texts describe the hamstring group as knee flexors, science now tells us that the hamstrings are actually powerful hip extensors and stabilizers of the knee. Hamstrings are only knee flexors in nonfunctional settings. In running, jumping, or skating, the function of the hamstrings and glutes is not to flex the knee but to extend the hip. As a result, lying or standing leg curls are generally a waste of time for athletes. Leg curls exercise the muscles in a pattern that is never used in sport. Training the muscles in nonfunctional patterns may explain the frequent recurrence of hamstring strains in athletes who rehabilitate with exercises such as leg curls or isokinetics. Stability-ball leg curls, which are illustrated later in this chapter, are an exception because this particular leg curl uses a closed-chain movement (foot in contact with a supporting surface).

Hip Extension Exercises

This section focuses on two distinct types of hip extension movements: straight-leg hip extensions and bent-leg hip extensions. It is critical to use exercises from both categories to properly train the posterior chain muscles (glutes and hamstrings). Although some experts claim that bent-leg hip extension isolates the glutes, I have not found this to be true for closed-chain movements. When the foot is in contact with a surface (stability ball or ground), both the glutes and hamstrings work to some degree. Both straight-leg hip extension and bent-leg hip extension target the glute and the hamstrings. It is not possible to eliminate one muscle group's contribution, only to lessen it. Straight-leg hip extension unquestionably targets the hamstrings to a greater degree, but I have found that all of the bent-leg hip extension exercises also involve the hamstrings.

It is important to note that knee flexion exercise such as squats and variations affect the glutes and hamstrings only as they relate to knee extension and hip extension to achieve a neutral standing position. To more fully involve the glutes and the hamstrings, the movement must be centered on the hip and not on the knee. To understand this concept, envision a front squat. The hip moves through an approximately 90-degree range of motion in concert with the knee movement. Generally there is one degree of hip movement for each degree of knee movement. The focus of the exercise is shared equally by the knee extensors and the hip extensors. In an exercise such as the modified straight-leg deadlift, the hip moves through a 90-degree range of motion, but the glutes are assisted by the hamstrings. A properly designed functional program must include both straight-leg, hip-dominant exercises and bent-leg, hip-dominant exercises to properly balance the lower-body muscles.

As in chapter 6, most of the exercises in this chapter use the 8-10-12 body-weight progression, meaning that only body weight is used for the first three weeks but the number of repetitions increases each week, from 8 to 10 to 12 reps.

Cook Hip Lift

Level 1

Noted physical therapist Gray Cook popularized this exercise to teach athletes how to separate the function of the hip extensors from the lumbar extensors. Most athletes are unaware of how little range of motion they possess in the hip joint when the range of motion in the lumbar spine is intentionally limited. To perform the movement, lie on the back with the feet flat on the floor (hook-lying position). Then place a tennis ball on the ribs and pull the knee to the chest hard enough to hold the tennis ball in place. From this position, push down through the foot on the floor and extend the hip while keeping the tennis ball tight against the ribs with the opposite leg (see figure 7.1). You will realize quickly that the range of motion in this exercise is only two to three inches. The range of motion can be increased significantly by relaxing the grip on the opposite knee, but this defeats the purpose. By relaxing the hold on the leg, you simply substitute lumbar spine extension for hip extension. This exercise has three distinct benefits.

1. The exercise uses the glutes and hamstrings as hip extensors.
2. The exercise teaches the athlete how to distinguish between hip extension and lumbar spine extension.
3. The coach or trainer can evaluate tightness in the hip flexor group that may be limiting hip extension and contributing to lower-back pain.

If you experience cramping in the hamstring, the glutes are not firing properly, and you should concentrate on the quadruped exercises in chapter 8 to develop better glute firing. Physical therapist Mike Clark of the National Academy of Sports Medicine uses this as an example of synergistic dominance, in which the hamstring is forced to compensate for a weak gluteus maximus.

Figure 7.1 Cook hip lift.

Hyperextension

Level 1 The hyperextension (figure 7.2) is possibly the worst-named exercise in the functional training toolbox. Hyperextensions may be referred to as back extensions or back raises, but whatever the name, they should be included in every beginning strength program. The hyperextension is a great basic exercise that teaches athletes to use the glutes and hamstrings as hip extensors. Despite the name, the emphasis should not be on hyperextending the lumbar spine but rather on using the glutes and hamstrings as hip extensors. The exercise has three major benefits.

1. It strengthens the posterior aspect of the trunk (spinal erectors); it works the low-back extensors in primarily an isometric, rather than concentric or eccentric, fashion. The spinal erectors (low-back muscles) are critical for maintaining proper position in all standing exercises.

2. It strengthens the glutes and hamstrings as hip extensors. Many people view the hyperextension as a lower-back exercise, but it is actually an excellent exercise for the upper hamstrings and glutes.

3. It promotes flexibility in the low back and hamstrings. The action of lowering and raising the weight of the torso stretches the hamstring group.

Use the body-weight progression, and then add weight by holding a plate at the chest or behind the head.

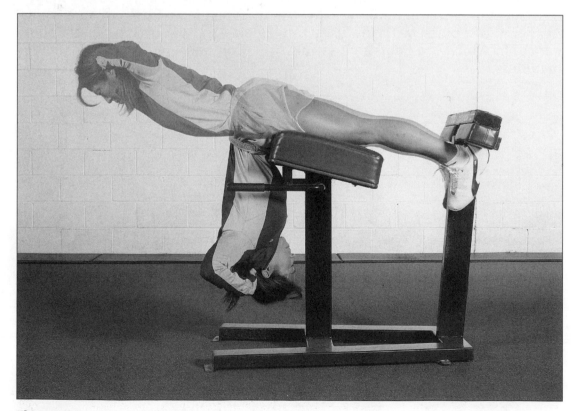

Figure 7.2 Hyperextension.

Hyperextension Hold

Hyperextension holds (hyper holds for short) are another variation of the hyperextension. Paul Chek, a noted strength and conditioning coach, first introduced this variation. Chek uses isometric hyperextension for clients with low-back pain, and we have incorporated this exercise into our training programs. Execution is simple. Perform one hyperextension, and hold the top position for 30 seconds initially, progressing to one minute. This stabilization exercise targets the glutes, hamstrings, and spinal erectors. Holding the arms out at 90 degrees to the body with the thumbs turned up also activates the thoracic extensors and rotator cuff.

Hold three sets of hyperextensions for 30 seconds in week 1, three sets for 45 seconds in week 2, and three sets for one minute in week 3.

Foot-Elevated Hip Lift

The foot-elevated hip lift is an excellent progression from the Cook hip lift; it has become a staple of our program. The foot can be elevated on an aerobic step, a balance board, a foam roller, or a medicine ball to increase the difficulty of the exercise. Aerobic steps in four-inch and six-inch heights allow a proper progression. For level 2 exercise, a four-inch step is used. For level 3, a six-inch step or balance board is used.

For level 4, a foam roller can be used. A two-dimensionally unstable surface such as a foam roller causes the hamstrings to be used in two separate but important functions. The hamstrings assist in hip extension while also working eccentrically to prevent knee extension.

To progress to level 5, a medicine ball can be used. The medicine ball is the most difficult due to the three-dimensional instability it introduces at the hip (see figure 7.3). The hamstrings must work at two joints, while the hip stabilizers work to prevent hip adduction and abduction.

For all these hip-lift exercises, use the 8-10-12 body-weight progression.

Figure 7.3 Foot-elevated hip lift using a medicine ball.

Modified Straight-Leg Deadlift

Level 2 The modified straight-leg deadlift (SLDL) ranks with the squat among frequently maligned, misunderstood, and poorly executed lifts. The squat and deadlift and their variations are often called unsafe and dangerous. In truth, these lifts are extremely safe and beneficial when performed correctly with an appropriate load. However, the squat and the SLDL can be dangerous when performed improperly or with too heavy a weight. The modified SLDL is performed with the legs slightly bent and the back arched. The SLDL, like the hyperextension, is an isometric exercise for the spinal erectors (lower-back muscles) and a concentric exercise for the hamstrings and glutes. It works the lower-back musculature similarly to the squat.

Please note that this is an extremely difficult lift to teach and should be learned with a dowel or weight bar prior to loading.

Technique Points

- For dumbbell SLDLs, the dumbbells are held with the palms in toward the thighs (neutral grip), and the hands should move down the outside of the thigh to the shin (see figure 7.4).

- For a straight bar, use a clean grip. Arms are straight. Wrists are curled under to encourage elbow extension.

- Feet should be approximately hip-width apart. Knees are slightly bent.

- Keep the back arched, the shoulder blades retracted, and the chest up.

- While maintaining your back position, slide the bar down the thighs until you reach the end of your *hamstring* range of motion.

The keys to the SLDL are bending from the hip and pushing the butt back while maintaining an arched back. Concentrate on pushing the hips and butt back, not on leaning forward. Athletes should start with the weight on the balls of the feet and, as they descend, shift their weight to the heels by pushing the butt back. Maintaining back position is important. Athletes must maintain at least a flat back. If they begin to flex the spine, they have reached the end of the active range of motion of the hamstrings. Remember that this is an isometric exercise for the spinal erectors and a concentric

Figure 7.4 Modified straight-leg deadlift.

exercise for the glutes and hamstrings. Movement should come from the hip, not from the lumbar spine.

Perform for multiple sets of 5 to 12 reps, depending on the level of training. Generally, no fewer than five reps should be done, as a precaution against back injury. Unless you are a power lifter, keep this lift light and do it with perfect technique.

One-Leg Straight-Leg Deadlift

The one-leg SLDL is a variation that develops the entire posterior chain (glutes and hamstrings) while also enhancing balance. This exercise is safe, challenging, and beneficial. One of the benefits is the tremendous proprioceptive work at the ankle. This exercise is preferred in our programs over the double-leg version. Single-leg hamstring work is always more functional than double-leg hamstring work, and single-leg hamstring work that challenges balance and proprioception is the most beneficial. Other pluses of the one-leg SLDL are that high loads are not necessary and the possibility of back injury is almost nonexistent. This is another exercise, like the lateral squat, that can be used as a body-weight warm-up or as a loaded strength exercise.

Technique Points

- The technique points for the modified SLDL apply.
- Due to the reduction in weight, back position is less critical than in the modified SLDL.
- One dumbbell is held in the hand opposite the supporting foot. Lean forward at the waist while lifting the free leg to the rear in line with the torso (figure 7.5).
- Attempt to place the dumbbell on the ground outside the opposite foot.

Do two to three sets of 5 to 12 reps per leg, depending on training level.

Figure 7.5 One-leg straight-leg deadlift.

One-Leg Hyperextension

Level 3 The one-leg hyperextension (figure 7.6) is a one-leg modification of the hyperextension. Using one leg significantly increases the difficulty and functional benefits of the exercise. When an athlete can perform 20 weighted hyperextensions, begin to use the single-leg version. From the standpoint of muscle function, this is a superior exercise because the athlete has to use one hamstring to extend the hip, as in running.

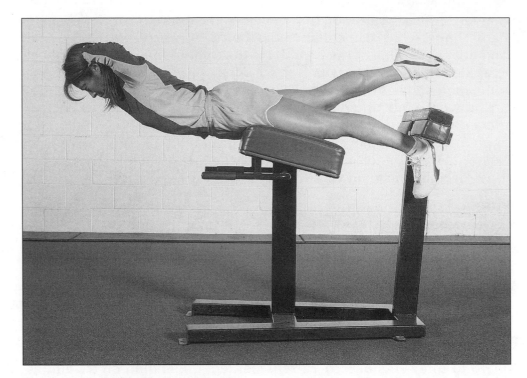

Figure 7.6 One-leg hyperextension.

Stability-Ball Hip Extension Variations

The stability ball allows closed-chain hamstring work with little or no risk to the low back, but beginner athletes often extend the lumbar spine with the lumbar extensors to give the appearance of hip movement. Athletes can use the stability ball in hip extension movements when they understand how to extend from the hip and not substitute lumbar extension for hip extension. The floor-based hip lifts described previously teach proper hip extension. These stability-ball variations are much more difficult to do properly than they appear and require practice. Emphasis should be on keeping the abdominals drawn in and using the hip extensors.

For all the following stability-ball exercises, follow the 8-10-12 body-weight progression.

Two-Leg Stability-Ball Hip Extension

Level 3 The stability-ball hip extension is a progression from the Cook hip lift and can be taught after it in the functional program. Generally a 65-centimeter stability ball is used. The stability-ball hip extension uses the hamstrings and glutes as hip extensors. It is extremely important that the movement come from the hips and not from extending the lumbar spine. You should understand the difference between hip range of motion and lumbar spine range of motion from mastering the Cook hip lift.

Technique Points

- Place the soles of the feet on the stability ball with hips and knees flexed to 90 degrees.
- Place the arms at the sides.
- Press the feet down onto the ball with the glutes and hamstrings.
- Raise the hips up until there is a straight line from the knees to the shoulders (see figure 7.7).
- Extend the hips, not the lumbar spine. Attempt to draw in the abdominals to stabilize the back.
- Think hip extension, not lumbar extension.

Figure 7.7 Two-leg stability-ball hip extension.

Stability-Ball Leg Curl

The stability-ball leg curl is a level 3 exercise because it requires using the glutes and spinal erectors to stabilize the torso and the hamstrings to perform a closed-chain leg curl. This exercise develops torso stability while also strengthening the hamstrings. The stability-ball leg curl is the only leg curl movement I recommend.

Technique Points

- Heels are placed on the ball, and the body is held with the hips off the ground.
- The ball is curled under the body with the heels while the body is kept straight (see figure 7.8).

Figure 7.8 Stability-ball leg curl.

One-Leg Stability-Ball Hip Extension

The one-leg stability-ball hip extension is a level 4 exercise because it is much more difficult than the two-leg version. Athletes who have not progressed through all the level 1, 2, and 3 exercises, particularly the foot-elevated hip lift, can get hamstring cramps or even hamstring strains if they attempt this exercise.

Technique Points

- Place the sole of one foot on the stability ball with the hip and knee flexed to 90 degrees.
- Place the arms at the sides.
- Push down into the ball with the foot to extend the hips.

One-Leg Stability-Ball Leg Curl

This is the same movement as the stability-ball leg curl only done with a single leg. This is an advanced exercise that can cause cramping in athletes with poor hamstring strength, so this exercise should not be used out of sequence.

Hybrid Exercises for Knee and Hip

Certain exercises cannot be categorized as knee dominant or hip dominant and thus are hybrid exercises. Although I do not recommend conventional deadlifts, they are an example of a hybrid exercise. The three hybrid exercises that athletes at our training facility do most frequently are the one-leg squat and touch, the skater's one-leg squat, and the trap-bar deadlift. In all these exercises the range of motion is split relatively evenly between the hip and the knee. These are great exercises for two-day workouts, as they work the entire functional scope of the lower extremity. In addition, these exercises are more positionally specific for sports like baseball, ice hockey, or field hockey that consistently place the athlete in a forward-flexed posture.

One-Leg Squat and Touch

For the one-leg squat and touch, stand on one foot with a dumbbell in the opposite hand. Then touch the dumbbell to the outside of the opposite foot (see figure 7.9). Bend at both the knee and the hip to combine the benefits of knee flexion and hip flexion. The exercise should not be done with a relatively upright torso as in the one-leg squat progression but neither should it be as forward flexed as the one-leg SLDL. The emphasis is more on sitting than leaning.

Do two to three sets of 5 to 12 reps, depending on level of training.

Figure 7.9 One-leg squat and touch.

Skater's One-Leg Squat

 The skater's one-leg squat is done in a single-leg stance on a 20- to 24-inch box (see figure 6.17 on page 68). As in the one-leg squat and touch, the athlete squats down until the rib cage contacts the thigh. This position combines knee flexion with hip flexion and the effects of the one-leg box squat with the effects of the one-leg SLDL.

Follow the 8-10-12 body-weight progression, and then add weight by means of a weighted vest.

Trap-Bar Deadlift

Level 3 The trap-bar deadlift is a hybrid exercise that is simple to teach and safer than the conventional deadlift due to the design of the bar. The diamond-shaped trap bar allows the athlete to crouch inside and simply stand up with the weight. Unlike in conventional deadlifts, stress can be kept off the back because the athlete can sit more than lean. The trap bar does not require keeping the bar close to the shins and thus eliminates many of the potential hazards of the conventional deadlift. The trap bar can also be used for straight-leg deadlifts.

Do three to five sets of 5 to 12 reps, depending on level of training.

Training the glutes and hamstrings as hip extensors rather than knee flexors goes a long way toward eliminating the hamstring strains so often seen in sport. Athletes and coaches are reminded to think about the true function of the muscles, not the anatomy-book description. Forget about hamstrings as knee flexors. See the hamstrings as powerful hip extensors and as muscles that eccentrically decelerate knee extension in running. Also remember to work the hamstrings and glutes with the knee flexed and the knee extended. This might be a major shift in thinking for some, but it will pay off in healthier hamstrings.

TARGETED TORSO TRAINING AND ROTATIONAL STRENGTH

One of the purposes of this book is to give you ideas that you can immediately put to use. The information in this chapter can improve the torso function of any athlete but is of particular interest to coaches and athletes involved in sports that place a great emphasis on trunk rotation. These exercises help develop a more stable platform from which to strike a ball, and the medicine-ball exercises improve the power and coordination of all the muscle groups used in striking skills. Torso training is the missing link to developing the power to hit a baseball or golf ball farther or a hockey puck or tennis ball harder and faster.

The word *torso* is intended to be broad and refers to all the muscles in the midsection. The torso muscles include the rectus abdominis (an abdominal muscle), the transversus abdominis (an abdominal muscle), the multifidus muscles (back muscles), the internal and external obliques (abdominal muscles), the quadratus lumborum (a low-back muscle), the spinal erectors (back muscles), and to a great extent, the gluteal, hamstring, and hip rotator groups (which cross the hip joint). You can't talk about training the torso without talking about training the spinal erectors, and you should train the spinal erectors in conjunction with the glutes and hamstrings. Current buzzwords used to describe torso training include ab work, core work, and power zone, but torso training is simple, descriptive, and more encompassing.

Why focus on the torso? Because the torso is the link between upper-body strength and lower-body strength, but it is often trained in an uninspired and unintelligent manner at the end of the workout. In the past very little time or energy was put into the development of proper programs for the torso. If there is a program at all, generally it consists of flexion-extension exercises for the rectus abdominis muscles such as crunches or sit-ups without addressing the need for a stable and powerful link from the lower body to the upper body. Unfortunately, torso training is done poorly mainly because it has always been done that way. Ask yourself how many sports involve flexion and extension of the trunk? The answer is very few. Sport is about stabilization and rotation.

The question of when to do torso work in the program is frequently debated. Those in favor of torso work at the end of the training program cite the possibility of fatiguing the muscles important to stability before the workout. I advocate doing torso work at the beginning of the strength program so that it will not be viewed as extra or unnecessary. Placing torso work at the beginning of the workout establishes the torso as a key area for sport training. The torso should be made a priority, and all torso work for abs, obliques, and so on (except some of the exercises that involve the spinal erectors, glutes, and hamstrings) should be done at the start of the workout. Resisted glute, hamstring, and spinal erector work should be done at the appropriate point in the workout on workout days focusing on the lower back and hamstrings. Athletes should generally not be allowed to touch a weight until all torso work is complete.

Torso training may not be fun. It doesn't work the "mirror" muscles as bench presses or curls do, but torso training is one of the keys to injury reduction and improved sport performance. People who train the torso are frequently more interested in visibly well-developed abs than in performance enhancement. But you should remember that a strong torso has nothing to do with low body fat. Abdominal definition is the result of diet, not torso work. Train your torso muscles to help you shoot harder, throw farther, or stay healthy longer.

Torso Training Basics

There are four basic functions of the torso muscles.

1. *Stabilization* is the primary function of the muscles of the torso and should be addressed in the first two to three phases of all programs. Stabilization is developed in three positions:
   a. Standing
   b. Bridging (feet and shoulders on the floor, knees bent to 90 degrees)
   c. Quadruped (on all fours)
2. *Lateral flexion* develops the quadratus lumborum as well as the obliques.
3. *Rotation* is the key to most sport skills, particularly striking a ball with an implement or throwing an object. Rotation is addressed by a rotational progression with body weight and with the medicine ball.
4. *Flexion* is an action that occurs rarely in sports.

Most programs generally require too much flexion and extension and not enough lateral flexion and stabilization work. Rotation with resistance is sometimes done, but rotation with velocity is frequently not addressed. The popularity of the stability ball has led to an increase in stabilization work, but it has not spread to enough programs. In some cases the stability ball has actually led to the use of exercises that are too advanced for the athletes. Stabilization work should be done initially on the floor to take advantage of the stable surface. This allows athletes to develop proper movement patterns. Remember that unstable surface training is a progression, not a place to start.

The best torso work is probably done in a sport-specific or, more appropriately, a sports-general position: standing. This makes medicine-ball throws and cable-column exercises probably the best overall torso exercises. Medicine-ball throws and standing cable-column exercises should be done at least as often as conventional abdominal work. (*Conventional* refers to exercises that are commonly considered abdominal or torso work, such as lateral flexion, stabilization, and flexion-extension exercises.)

Advantages of Medicine-Ball Training

- The medicine ball allows the user to work in a sports-general position or pattern. These patterns are similar to the golf swing, tennis swing, baseball swing, and numerous other striking skills.
- Medicine balls bridge the gap from conventional strength and endurance exercises for the torso to power development for the torso. Think of medicine-ball work as plyometrics for the torso. The medicine ball allows the muscles to contract at speed similar to that encountered in sports.
- The medicine ball teaches summation of force, from the ground through the legs, through the torso, and finally out through the arms. This is the essence of torso function. The athlete learns to transfer force from the ground to the ball, with the torso as the vital link.
- Medicine-ball training can be done alone if a concrete block wall is available.
- Work with the medicine ball has a total-body conditioning effect.

Disadvantages of Medicine-Ball Training

- You don't feel it. Athletes often judge torso work by the "burn." You do not feel the effect of medicine-ball training until the next day.
- You need space. Medicine-ball training takes up a large amount of space and requires masonry walls to throw against.
- Coaches need lots of medicine balls in a range of sizes.

Advantages of Cable-Column Training

- Cable-column torso work is done in a standing position.
- Cable-column torso work allows you to progress from stabilization exercises to dynamic resisted exercises.
- Cable columns allow the use of progressive resistance in torso exercise.

Disadvantages of Cable-Column Training

- The equipment is costly.
- Exercises such as the chop and lift are not easy to teach or learn and require time and energy from coaches and athletes.
- There is often psychological resistance to any new concept. The idea of doing ab work while standing with primary emphasis on isometric stabilization is a tough concept to sell to some athletes and coaches.

Organizing Torso Training in the Weekly Program

The distribution of weekly torso training should be done as follows: For two-day programs or in-season programs, combine both medicine-ball throwing and conventional abdominal exercises in the same day's workout. Each session should include one or two medicine-ball exercises and one or two conventional abdominal exercises.

In a three-day program, use an ABA pattern one week and a BAB the next week, alternating a medicine-ball day (A) with a conventional abdominal day (B) for a total of three medicine-ball workouts and three conventional abdominal workouts over a two-week period.

In a four-day program, alternate conventional abdominal work on one day with medicine-ball work on the next day for a total of two medicine-ball days and two conventional days per week.

How to progress torso work is a difficult subject, but progression must be done in the program. Three sets of 8 to 12 repetitions of most conventional abdominal exercises are done initially. Rotation and lateral flexion exercises are done 10 times on each side. Stabilization exercises generally start with three sets of 15 seconds' duration. Stabilization exercises that require alternating from right to left are held isometrically for five seconds before changing positions. Physical therapist Al Visnick introduced this concept to me with the statement: "If you want to train the stabilizers, you have to give them time to stabilize." One-second holds cannot work the stabilizers as effectively as a five-second contraction. You can use time instead of reps to determine the length of set. Twelve reps take approximately one minute. These are general guidelines and can be adjusted based on the athlete's age and experience.

For any exercise using body weight, progress over a three-week period as follows:

Week 1: 3 × 8

Week 2: 3 × 10

Week 3: 3 × 12

After week 3, progress to a slightly more difficult version of the exercise, reduce the number of repetitions, and again follow the same progression.

Remember that torso work must be taught and coached like any other portion of a program. Simply doing torso work at the beginning of the strength program rather than leaving it until the end is not enough. Coaches should teach torso work as well as or better than any other facet of the program. A properly taught torso program aids in injury reduction, strength improvement, and speed improvement by improving the ability to maintain trunk position in strength exercises, jumps, and sprints. In addition, a well-designed torso program can markedly improve performance in striking sports. These benefits cannot be overstated.

Learning to Draw In

At a 1999 Perform Better functional training clinic, I had the pleasure of listening to Mike Clark, a well-respected physical therapist, discuss abdominal training. I must confess that I left a little bit confused. The gist of the presentation was "You're doing all of your abdominal training wrong."

I soon realized that, based on new research findings coming primarily out of Australia, we had inadvertently fallen behind in training methods for the abdominal area. After we had established that we were doing everything wrong, I asked a simple question: What do we do now? At the time Mike Clark had great information but not enough answers for me. Mike's explanation of the new Australian research revolved around this idea: "You need to teach your athletes to use their transverse abdominis to draw in their abs." As I researched and read, the problem became a bit clearer. To begin, a little anatomical background is necessary. The transversus abdominis was previously regarded as a little-used, deep abdominal muscle that rated about two lines in my 1974 copy of *Gray's Anatomy*. In fact, the muscle was referred to as the transversalis and was basically ignored in the book. Australian researchers Richardson, Jull, Hodges, and Hides (1999) have reported that the transversus abdominis and the multifidus (another muscle ignored in my ancient text) are potential keys to unlocking the cure for back pain. The research shows that the transversus abdominis is the first muscle recruited when almost any limb movement occurs. More important, the transversus abdominis and internal oblique are the only abdominal muscles that originate on the thoracolumbar fascia (connective tissue of the spine) and can therefore serve as a natural "weight belt" to resist flexion of the lumbar spine. Although I believed what Mike had said, I still was left with the quandary, What actually is "drawing in," and how do I teach 300 athletes to draw in?

The beginning of the answer came from a magazine for pregnant women. Physical therapists who work with pregnant and postpartum women have been very creative in teaching them to use the deep abdominal muscles, long before those in the athletic world even considered the concept. These therapists realized the importance of using and strengthening the transversus abdominis for both childbirth and postpartum recovery.

For most athletes, learning to draw in the abdominals is a difficult process. For the vast majority of athletes, abdominal training has involved flexion and extension movements that focus almost exclusively on the rectus abdominis. Stabilization or flexion of the torso is often achieved by shortening the rectus abdominis and in effect pushing out the abdomen. The concept of drawing in is the exact opposite and results in a different emphasis in almost all of the torso exercises. The new Australian research explains why athletes with abdominal musculature that appears thick and strong can still exhibit extreme lordotic posture (forward curvature of the spine) and be plagued by low-back pain. For years many coaches and athletes have been training the wrong muscle. The rectus abdominis runs from the rib cage to the middle of the pubic bone and cannot act on the lumbar spine. Contraction of the rectus abdominis can only tilt the pelvis backward, not flatten the lumbar spine.

A number of exercises can be used to teach athletes to draw in the abdominals. No single exercise seems to work best for everyone. I therefore include five exercises that teach drawing in from different positions: lying draw-in, quadruped draw-in, kneeling overhead draw-in, prone draw-in, and standing draw-in. I also offer progressions or variations of these. Remember that drawing in the abdominals is a difficult movement to teach; the visualizations and props suggested later can speed the learning process.

Recent work by Dr. Stuart McGill (2002) has raised some eyebrows. McGill, a noted expert on the lumbar spine, has proposed "bracing" rather than drawing in. McGill makes a great case for bracing as a co-contraction of the deep abdominals and rectus abdominis; however, I feel it is important to train the deep abdominal muscles that athletes have not trained for years and try to discourage rectus abdominis overuse. In fact, both approaches have the same goal: increased stability of the lumbar spine through development of the deep abdominals. Whether you favor draw-ins or bracing, you are on the right track.

All the draw-in exercises are level 1 exercises. It may take athletes four to six weeks to understand the concept and learn to execute the exercises. Athletes who get daily individual instruction will generally learn most quickly; groups will take longer. Any athlete who has done lots of conventional crunches and sit-ups may struggle to learn the draw-in action. These "rectus-dominant" athletes consistently activate the rectus abdominis and push out the abdominal wall. Athletes with a background in yoga, Pilates, or martial arts usually find these exercises simpler.

Lying Draw-In

The lying draw-in is the simplest exercise for most beginners to learn to draw in the abdominal muscles. In this exercise, two hockey pucks taped together visually reinforce the action of drawing in. Lie on the back with the head supported on a foam roller and an additional roller between the knees. The pucks should be placed in line with the hip bones. The roller under the head allows you to see the pucks, to relax the rectus abdominis, and to focus on the action of the transversus abdominis. The roller between the knees teaches you to use the adductor musculature and involve the pelvic floor more. Squeeze the roller between the knees, and then attempt to draw the pucks down into the abdomen *without* initiating a crunching action (see figure 8.1). The point is to learn to fire the transversus abdominis without firing the rectus abdominis. Use one of these visualizations to help draw in the abdomen.

1. Attempt to pull the bellybutton through to the spine.
2. Visualize trying to squeeze through a tight space between two objects at waist height.
3. Imagine trying to zip up the world's tightest pair of pants.

A level 1 exercise set consists of five reps, each held for five seconds. Relax and let the puck rise for two to three seconds between reps. Do three sets. For a level 2 exercise, do three sets of eight contractions held for five seconds.

Figure 8.1   Lying draw-in.

Quadruped Draw-In

Level 1

Another method of teaching drawing in begins with the athlete on all fours. In this position, which I call the quadruped, the internal organs weigh down against the rectus abdominis. The athlete pulls the abdominal wall toward the spine without arching the back (figure 8.2). Athletes also attempt to exhale as they draw in. A 12- to 18-inch piece of foam roller can be squeezed between the knees to involve the adductor musculature. The adductor muscles share with the abdominals a common attachment on the mid pubic bone. Squeezing the roller enhances the contraction of the entire pelvic floor area. This tip, along with the following exercise, is courtesy of physical therapist Gray Cook.

Use same progression as for the lying draw-in.

Figure 8.2 Quadruped draw-in.

Kneeling Overhead Draw-In

Level 1 The kneeling overhead draw-in is an excellent exercise for three reasons:

1. It provides a natural progression from all fours to a slightly more functional kneeling position.

2. It is easy to cue by asking the athlete to get as tall as possible. It is natural to incorporate the deep abdominal musculature to elongate the trunk.

3. The overhead draw-in works as a reflex. Envision trying to put a box up on a shelf that you can't quite reach. As you try to reach the last inch, the deep abdominal musculature reflexively kicks in to give you that extra inch.

Place a foam roller between the knees and use a medicine ball overhead for resistance (figure 8.3). You can progress from medicine balls to actual weight plates. Our athletes lift as much as 45 pounds in this exercise.

Do three sets of five contractions held for five seconds.

Figure 8.3 Kneeling overhead draw-in.

Prone Draw-In

 Level 1

The prone draw-in is another exercise that helps teach the draw-in. Lie face down on a tennis ball at the level of the navel or slightly below, in line with the hips, and simply lift the abdominal wall off the ball (figure 8.4). Don't lift the hips, just the abdominal wall.

Do three sets of five contractions held for five seconds.

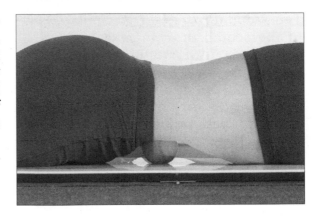

Figure 8.4 Prone draw-in.

Seated Draw-In

Level 1

To do the seated draw-in, sit on a stability ball. Wrap a 48-inch length of rope around the waist, and hold one end in each hand, as shown in figure 8.5. From this position, try to draw in the abdomen away from the rope. Make yourself as tall and thin as possible. Use the rope to reinforce the draw-in action.

Figure 8.5 Seated draw-in.

Standing Draw-In

Level 1
The standing draw-in is similar to the seated draw-in, except it is done from a standing position (figure 8.6). This is the most functional position to work in. As you draw in, gently pull the rope wrapped around your waist tighter. Think "tall and thin." Some athletes grasp the draw-in concept most easily with this exercise. This exercise seems to work well in groups, unlike some of the other draw-in exercises.

Figure 8.6 Standing draw-in.

Standing Draw-In With Hip Flexion

Level 1
While standing and drawing in the abdominal muscles, attempt to bring one knee to waist height. The deep abdominals must maintain an isometric contraction while 10 hip flexions are performed. A rope wrapped around the waist reinforces the draw-in.

Integrating Draw-In Maneuvers With Movement

I had an important realization as I tried to integrate movement into the draw-in exercises. In developing torso programs, like many other coaches, I had experimented with what are commonly referred to as "dead bug" or "dying bug" exercises (so named because of the supine position in which they are executed). Until I began to understand the function of the deep abdominal stabilizers and the concept of drawing in, these dead bug exercises seemed to be ineffective. Athletes could perform hundreds of reps with very little fatigue, and what fatigue they did feel was most often in the hip flexors.

At first I thought that our highly trained clients would make the transition simply and quickly from exercises such the lying draw-in to using the draw-in in an unsupported dead bug movement. This could not have been more wrong. As soon as movement was added, the athletes could no longer isometrically control the movement of their pelvis. We experimented initially with a simple bicycling movement (supine alternate leg extension) that should have been easy. None of the athletes possessed enough deep abdominal control to execute this movement. This led us back to the dead bug exercises. The work of Dr. Watkins (1996) made it obvious why they progressed from a position with the feet supported on the floor to an unsupported position with the hips flexed 90 degrees. The supported position allows the athlete to stress the deep abdominal area with a minimum of movement. Over the past year I have experimented with the following progression to integrate drawing in the abdominals with limb movement. This progression allows athletes to drastically increase the load on the deep abdominal muscles while performing the exercises properly.

Knee Fallouts

 Level 2

Knee fallouts are a way to integrate movement and the isometric action of drawing in the abdominals without overwhelming the lumbar spine with the powerful hip flexor musculature. The well-developed hip flexors of most athletes make it difficult for them to add movement to dead bug exercises. In the knee fallout, the abduction-adduction movement incorporates the action of the adductors with the stabilization of the transversus abdominis and internal oblique.

Lie on the back and perform the lying draw-in with a roller under the head but no roller between the knees. From this position, let the knees "fall out" while maintaining the drawn-in abdomen (see figure 8.7). The draw-in is isometrically maintained for 10 reps. If it seems easy, the transversus contraction is probably not

Figure 8.7 Knee fallouts.

being maintained. The coach should be able to see both the strain and the concentration on the athlete's face. The exercise should seem somewhat mechanical; concentrate on keeping the abdominals drawn in. Follow the body-weight progression of 10 reps in week 1, 12 in week 2, and 14 in week 3.

Single-Knee Fallouts

Follow the same instructions as for knee fallouts, but move one leg at a time.

Lying Draw-In With Hip Flexion (Feet Supported)

This exercise is the first of the dead bug exercises. In this version of the lying draw-in with hip flexion, isometrically hold the lying draw-in position with hockey pucks resting on the abdomen, and then flex the hip to lift the foot off the ground (figure 8.8). If you can do it easily, you are doing it wrong. It should be difficult for most athletes. The coach should be able to see both the strain and the concentration on the athlete's face, as in knee fallouts. The opposite foot must stay on the ground to further support the pelvis. The coach should place a hand under the athlete's low back to ensure that there is no space. When this exercise is properly executed, the space between the lumbar spine and the floor should disappear. The key is to make the space disappear by activating the deep abdominals and not by using the rectus abdominis to create a backward pelvic tilt.

Figure 8.8 Lying draw-in with hip flexion (feet supported).

Lying Draw-In With Hip Flexion (Feet Unsupported)

Level
3

In this version of the lying draw-in with hip flexion, isometrically hold the lying draw-in position with hockey pucks resting on the abdomen, the knees bent 90 degrees, and the hips flexed 90 degrees so that the feet are not touching the ground (figure 8.9). This is a major change in stress and stability from earlier lying draw-in exercises; it is much easier to stabilize with the feet supported than unsupported. Lower one foot to touch the floor while maintaining the isometric draw-in. If you can do it easily, you are doing it wrong. This should be a somewhat difficult progression from the previous feet-supported version for most athletes. The coach should be able to see both the strain and the concentration on the athlete's face.

Figure 8.9 Lying draw-in with hip flexion (feet unsupported).

Lying Draw-In With Hip Flexion and Extension (Feet Unsupported)

Level 3 To do the lying draw-in with hip flexion and extension, isometrically hold the lying draw-in position with hockey pucks on the abdomen, knees bent 90 degrees, and feet off the ground. Then flex and extend the hip (figure 8.10). Extend the leg only as far as you can while still holding the pucks down in the drawn-in position. This is a subtle but difficult progression from the previous version with only hip extension because of the leverage added by extending the leg. The pull of the hip flexors on the lumbar spine is much greater when the leg is extended. As with all the preceding lying draw-in exercises, if you can do it easily, you are doing it wrong.

Figure 8.10 Lying draw-in with hip flexion and extension (feet unsupported).

Dead Bug

Level 3 The dead bug is the final step in the progression. Both arms and legs are off the floor while drawing in the abdominals (see figure 8.11). This is difficult and requires a great deal of concentration. The coach should check the space

Figure 8.11 Dead bug.

under the athlete's lower back and continually monitor facial expression for effort and concentration. These exercises should never look easy. These draw-in exercises with movement are not effective in group settings; teaching needs to be one on one with constant monitoring for an athlete to master these exercises. Coaching these exercises has made me appreciate how difficult it is to teach a supine progression.

Combination Draw-In and Flexion-Extension Exercises

In abdominal programs at our training facility, draw-in exercises initially take the place of flexion-extension exercises. Because of the dominance of the rectus abdominis in most athletes, ensure that the transversus abdominis can function independently of the rectus abdominis before introducing combination draw-in and flexion-extension exercises. The progression takes at least nine weeks. In these exercises, the pelvis stays fixed, and the shoulder girdle moves toward the pelvis. The degree of trunk flexion is drastically reduced by the draw-in action. (Remember, the transversus abdominis has a strong antiflexion effect.) If you can do a draw-in crunch easily, you are doing it incorrectly. Most athletes have difficulty maintaining the draw-in action while simultaneously recruiting the rectus abdominis in a simple crunch. Eventually progress back to the same flexion-extension exercises but with a constant draw-in.

Draw-In Crunch

 Level 4

The draw-in crunch (figure 8.12) is the first exercise to learn that combines abdominal drawing-in with conventional torso flexion and extension. The draw-in crunch combines the lying draw-in with a short-range crunch. The key is to maintain the draw-in action while initiating a crunch. This is not a simple task. If you can do it easily, you are probably not maintaining the draw-in. The key is to draw in, hold the position, and then activate the rectus.

Begin with 10 five-second holds for one set of 50 seconds, and progress to 12 and then 14 five-second holds. Only one set is needed.

Figure 8.12 Draw-in crunch.

Straight-Leg Draw-In Crunch

The straight-leg draw-in crunch is the same as the previous draw-in crunch but with straight legs. This advanced flexion-extension exercise should be used in limited amounts only after the draw-in is mastered.

Begin with 10 five-second holds for one set of 50 seconds, and progress to 12 and then 14 five-second holds. Only one set is needed.

Extended Draw-In Crunch

The extended draw-in crunch (figure 8.13) is another advanced flexion-extension exercise to introduce when athletes have mastered the draw-in. The emphasis should always be on drawing in first and then executing a short-range crunch that activates both the transversus abdominis and the rectus abdominis. Be sure that the ball height allows the athlete to get the hips and shoulders on approximately the same level at the start. This is a great advanced exercise that should be saved for well-trained athletes. The extended range of motion makes this the most difficult of these combined exercises.

Begin with 10 five-second holds for one set of 50 seconds, and progress to 12 and then 14 five-second holds. Only one set is needed.

Figure 8.13 Extended draw-in crunch.

Stick Crunch

The stick crunch (figure 8.14) is another difficult flexion-extension exercise and one that appears to be contrary to the functional philosophy. The stick crunch is the only conventional sit-up-type exercise that I recommend. It has numerous variations: reverse crunch (shoulders stay down, feet come under the stick), total crunch (both hips and shoulders leave the floor), or a regular crunch (shoulders off the ground). The athlete must make a concerted effort to get the stick past the feet. This is an easy-to-evaluate abdominal exercise: Either the stick gets over the toes or it doesn't. Athletes feel this movement like very few others because of the well-defined end point (i.e., the stick past the feet). One benefit of the stick crunch is the development of shoulder blade and hip mobility from reaching to get the stick over the feet. Although many athletes complain of the difficulty of this exercise, most can master it. The stick crunch is a rectus dominant exercise and should be used sparingly. Follow the body-weight progression of 3 × 10, 12, 14.

Figure 8.14 Stick crunch.

Supine Progression

The supine progression may be the most important part of the overall torso training program for two reasons. First, athletes generally ignore these exercises, which they tend to view as back or hamstring exercises and therefore less important for injury prevention. Many athletes believe that the key to a healthy back is to train the muscles in the front. The supine progression targets the back from the spine through the multifidus.

Second, the supine exercises train or retrain the multifidus. The multifidus, along with the transversus abdominis, has received much attention recently due to research being conducted in Australia. This research has shown that the multifidus and transversus abdominis experience rapid atrophy after back injury and must be retrained by any athlete who has experienced back pain. The multifidus muscles are the deepest of the spinal erector group but are not responsible for extension. Instead, they are responsible for rotational stability between individual vertebrae. To exercise the multifidus muscles, rotational stress must be applied to the spine. Training or retraining the multifidus muscles is often neglected in many torso and low-back rehabilitation programs. Although great attention has been lavished on the deep abdominal musculature, the ability to stabilize the spinal column itself is potentially more important. The supine progression teaches the movement patterns necessary to safely and correctly perform supine exercises and thus to target the multifidus.

Cook Hip Lift

Level 1
This is a level 1 exercise with dual emphasis on glutes and hamstrings and on the torso. The Cook hip lift was discussed in chapter 7 (page 75). It develops glute and hamstring strength, but, more importantly, it teaches the critical difference between hip range of motion and lumbar spine range of motion. This is an important goal of all the supine exercises. In many exercises that target the hamstrings and glutes, it is easy to mistakenly use more range of motion at the lumbar spine than at the hip.

To perform the Cook hip lift, lie on the back in the hook-lying position, then pull one knee tightly to the chest to limit movement at the lumbar spine. To ensure that the knee stays tight against the chest, place a tennis ball near the bottom of the rib cage and pull the thigh up to hold the ball in place. The ball must not fall out during the set. The opposite knee is bent 90 degrees, and the foot is flat on the floor. Extend the hip by pushing the foot down into the floor. Don't be surprised if the range of motion is limited initially to a few degrees. This exercise has two purposes:

1. It teaches the difference between range of motion of the hip and range of motion of the lumbar spine.

2. You can get some additional flexibility in the psoas due to the reciprocal nature of the exercise. You can't contract the glute and hamstring without relaxing the psoas.

Follow the body-weight progression, 3 × 10, 12, 14 reps on each leg.

Isometric Supine Bridge

Level 1
This level 1 exercise requires that the athlete transfer the knowledge gained about hip range of motion from the Cook hip lift to a bridge position. Begin in a hook-lying position, and raise the hips to create a straight line from the knee through the hip to the shoulder (see figure 8.15). You must create and maintain this posture by using the glutes and hamstrings, not by extending the lumbar spine. Any drop in the hips drastically reduces the effectiveness of the exercise. At the top point, draw in the abdominals and simply maintain this position. Before attempting this exercise, it is important to learn the difference between hip movement and lumbar spine movement through an exercise such as the Cook hip lift. Most athletes who do not understand this distinction arch the back to attempt to extend the hip.

Do three 30-second holds.

Figure 8.15 Isometric supine bridge.

Isometric Single-Leg Supine Bridge

Level 2

To do the isometric single-leg supine bridge, begin in a hook-lying position, but extend one leg off the ground and raise the hips to create a straight line from the knee through the hip to the shoulder (see figure 8.16). Then draw in the abdominals and simply maintain this single-leg position by pushing the foot down and squeezing the glutes. Squeeze the glutes as if you were trying to make a hard fist.

Do three 15-second holds on each side.

Figure 8.16 Isometric single-leg supine bridge.

Bridge With Alternate March

Level 3 The next step in the progression is to add a small alternate march action to the isometric bridge. You simply alternate lifting one foot then the other off the ground. A yardstick across the crests of the hip bones acts as a level to remind you not to let the opposite hip drop when the foot is lifted. With this exercise the progression begins to truly target the multifidus, due to the rotational stress applied to the spinal column as a result of moving from four support points (shoulders and feet) to three support points (shoulders and one foot). Push down through the heel and activate the glute on the same side as the supporting foot. See figure 8.17.

Do one set of 10 five-second holds (5 on each leg). Progress to 12 and then 14 holds.

Figure 8.17 Bridge with alternative march.

Quadruped Progression

The quadruped exercises are frequently viewed as rehabilitation exercises and have largely been ignored by strength and conditioning coaches and athletic trainers. I believe that this is largely due to the old theory that strong abs mean a healthy back. Like the supine progression, the quadruped exercises may not make sense at first glance, but only because these exercises are often performed incorrectly. In many cases the results of these exercises become the opposite of what was intended. Quadruped exercises should teach athletes how to recruit the glutes and hamstrings while maintaining a stable torso. Instead, athletes often learn that they can mimic hip extension by extending (or hyperextending) the lumbar spine. The purpose of this quadruped progression is to teach the athlete to stabilize the torso with the deep abdominals and multifidus muscles and to simultaneously use the hip extensors to extend the hip. A great deal of low-back pain is related to poor range of motion and function of the hip that must be compensated for by lumbar extension or rotation.

Quadruped Draw-In

Level 1 Follow the same technique as described on page 91. Start on all fours, and exhale as you draw in the abdomen. Squeeze a 12- to 18-inch piece of foam roller between the knees to involve the adductor musculature. Squeezing the roller enhances the contraction of the entire pelvic floor area.

Quadruped Hip Extension: Straight Leg, Dowel Parallel

Level 1 The quadruped hip extension progression is simple. Initially you extend the hip and knee and hold the position for five seconds before alternating sides. In level 1, this is done while balancing a dowel or stick along the spine. The objective sounds simple, but it is actually difficult to accomplish. Extend the leg without disturbing the dowel or allowing the lumbar spine to move away from the dowel (figure 8.18). Any change in lumbar curve can easily be seen as an increase in the space between the dowel and the lumbar spine. With proper control of the lumbar spine via the deep abdominals and multifidus muscles, the hip should extend without extension of the lumbar spine.

Progress from 10 to 12 and then to 14 five-second holds.

Figure 8.18 Quadruped hip extension: straight leg, dowel parallel.

Functional Training for Sports

Quadruped Hip Extension: Straight Leg, Dowel Perpendicular

 Level 2 After you master the straight-leg version of the quadruped hip extension with the dowel parallel to the spine, the dowel is shifted to a position perpendicular to the spine, over the hip bones (see figure 8.19). The same hip and knee extension is performed, but now the objective is to eliminate any rotational compensation in the lumbar spine.

Figure 8.19 Quadruped hip extension: straight leg, dowel perpendicular.

Quadruped Hip Extension: Bent Leg, Dowel Parallel

Level 3 In the level 3 progression of the quadruped hip extension, the dowel is again parallel to the spine, but instead of extending the hip and knee to a straight-leg position, the leg is extended with the knee bent to further isolate the glutes.

Quadruped Hip Extension: Bent Leg, Dowel Perpendicular

Level 4 In the level 4 progression, the leg is extended at the hip with the knee bent and the dowel perpendicular to the spine.

106

Quadruped Alternating Arm and Leg

Level 4 Now add an alternate arm and leg action to the quadruped hip extension (figure 8.20). This is an advanced exercise that is often done poorly by beginners.
All the preceding exercises are held for five seconds and progress using the 10-12-14 body-weight progression.

Figure 8.20 Quadruped alternating arm and leg.

Hips-to-Shoulders Flexion-Extension Exercises

In addition to exercises that bring the shoulders toward the hips, you can occasionally include exercises that move the hips toward the shoulders. As you have seen, the torso musculature can perform numerous actions other than the conventional crunch and sit-up movements. These exercises are reserved for athletes who have excellent draw-in capability and are looking for a greater challenge.

Hip Thrusts and Five-Second Isometric Hip Thrusts

 Level 4 This exercise has two variations. Hip thrusts are short-range movements that put stress on the lower rectus abdominis. Press the soles of the feet up to the ceiling in a slow and controlled manner (figure 8.21). No swinging or swaying is allowed. This is a difficult movement for athletes to learn. In the five-second isometric version, the top position is held for five seconds, and five reps are done.

Figure 8.21 Hip thrusts.

Ball Reverse Crunch

 Level 4 The ball reverse crunch is another hips-to-shoulders exercise. Hold a stability ball with the feet and hamstrings, and roll the knees up toward the chest (see figure 8.22). Then slowly lower the ball back to the floor or mat. Please be aware that most of these exercises are intended to work the lower abdominals, but the deep abdominal work is of greater importance.

Follow the body-weight progression 3 × 10, 12, 14.

Figure 8.22 Ball reverse crunch.

Lateral Flexion Exercises

Lateral flexion exercises are frequently neglected in torso training programs. Lateral flexion exercises target the quadratus lumborum and the obliques and help to provide a solid cylinder in combination with the transversus, rectus, and erector group.

Oblique Bridge

The oblique bridge is actually a misnomer, as most of the bridging exercises in this book are isometric in nature. In the oblique bridge the trunk moves through lateral flexion with two supporting points—the feet and the elbows—on the ground. Simply lower the hips until they barely touch the ground, and then bring the hips up to a position above the neutral starting position (see figure 8.23). It is critical that you keep the body in a straight line from head to toe and laterally flex without rotation.

Follow the body-weight progression.

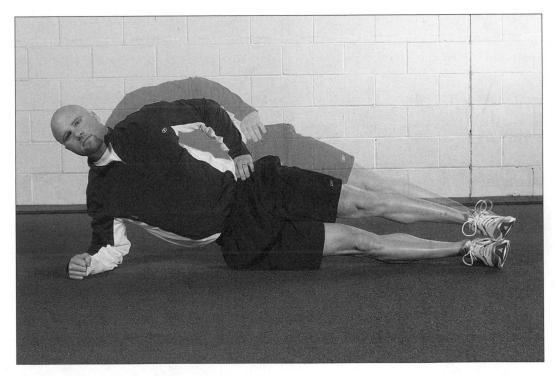

Figure 8.23   Oblique bridge.

Off-Bench Oblique

The off-bench oblique is an excellent lateral flexion exercise but should be preceded by the oblique bridge or the four-point stability series (given later in this chapter) for at least a few workouts. Off-bench obliques produce great soreness in the quadratus after the first workout. Start with one to two sets of 10 on each side. Emphasize full range without rotation. This exercise should use pure lateral flexion in the frontal plane only. Weak athletes compensate with the rectus and introduce rotation. Off-bench obliques can be progressed as follows:

1. Hands crossed in front of the body (level 1). See figure 8.24.
2. Hands behind the head (level 2)
3. Arms extended overhead with stick (level 3)

In this progression the lever arm is gradually lengthened, adding to the difficulty of the exercise.

Follow a nine-week body-weight progression: level 1, 3 × 10, 12, 14; level 2, 3 × 10, 12, 14; then level 3, 3 × 10, 12, 14.

Figure 8.24 Off-bench oblique.

Stabilization Exercises

Stabilization exercises were formerly the realm of the physical therapist. Coaches took a long time to see the importance of the torso muscles as stabilizers. I contend that physical therapists are two or three years ahead of strength and conditioning coaches in the application of new concepts. Lumbar stabilization has been utilized in physical therapy for years to treat low-back dysfunction, but only recently has stabilization come to be seen as a preventive measure for any athlete. Ask yourself two questions:

1. What is the primary function of the torso in most strength training exercises? The answer is stabilization.

2. How much time is spent training the torso muscles as stabilizers? In most programs, very little.

Try to include at least one lumbar stabilization exercise in each non-medicine-ball workout. These exercises are drawn from the bridging exercises, the quadruped exercises discussed earlier in this chapter, or the stabilization exercises that follow. Stabilization exercises are held for two to three sets of 30 seconds. Progression can be achieved by increasing the time of the isometric contraction to 45 seconds, by using a single-leg stance, or by doing the exercises in a minicircuit.

The only difference between the stabilization exercises presented here and the conventional ones is that these use abdominal draw-in rather than a pelvic tilt or a neutral pelvis. I feel that both tilted and neutral pelvis positions are outdated and nonfunctional. The emphasis should be on learning to turn on the deep abdominal muscles, not to use more rectus abdominis activation. Stabilization is neither easy nor natural. Teaching an athlete to properly stabilize the spine through contraction of the deep abdominals requires constant reinforcement.

Push-Up Bridge

The push-up bridge is a simple, isometric abdominal exercise that also works the scapular stabilizers. As in all stabilization exercises, draw in the deep abdominals; do not crunch and activate the rectus abdominis. Keep the hips level with the floor. This exercise can be done with a balance board or stability ball (see figure 8.25).

Figure 8.25 Push-up bridge.

Shoulder Bridge

The shoulder bridge is similar to the push-up bridge, but the unstable surface is moved from under the hands to under the feet (see figure 8.26). The shoulder bridge places greater proprioceptive demand on the shoulder stabilizers. All other techniques and cues remain the same. For many athletes this is the more difficult exercise.

Figure 8.26   Shoulder bridge.

Back Bridge

The back bridge is another simple stabilization exercise. Place the shoulders on a stability ball, and place a 12- to 18-inch piece of foam roller between the knees (figure 8.27). Activate the glutes, hamstrings, and adductors while contracting the deep abdominals. A wide base allows the iliotibial bands and lateral quadriceps of the thighs to aid in stabilization.

Figure 8.27   Back bridge.

Bridge Circuit

Advanced athletes can do a circuit of push-up to shoulder to back bridge, allowing only enough time to change positions.

Four-Point Stabilization Series

The four-point stabilization series of exercises currently serves as the starting point for many of our conventional torso programs. A number of progressions can be devised from these simple but effective exercises. If you would like to add stabilization training to your program but you do not have enough stability balls, the four-point stabilization series is an excellent alternative. Progress from a push-up position to a side-support position on the right elbow to a rear-support position and finally to a side-support position on the left elbow (see figure 8.28). Start with 20 seconds in each position. This physically demanding series requires constant feedback from the coach.

Figure 8.28 Four-point stabilization series.

Cable Column Standing Chop

The chop and the lift were introduced by nationally recognized physical therapist and Reebok University consultant Gray Cook (1997). Cook advocated diagonal patterns of trunk flexion with rotation (chop) and trunk extension with rotation (lift). Cook has since modified his original versions so that the chop and lift exercises are exercises in which the arms transfer force on a diagonal through a stable torso. The chop and lift exercises presented here have been modified from Cook's. These exercises challenge trunk stability through the use of a cable column. To properly perform these exercises, a special handle, a 20-inch-long bar fitted with an eyehook, is needed for the cable column. These handles can be obtained from Samson Equipment (800-4SAMSON).

To do the standing chop, stand at the cable column, grasp the handle with hands approximately 12 to 14 inches apart, pull to the waist, and then press down without altering the position of the torso (see figure 8.29). Watch for hips shifting right or left or for inability to stabilize the scapula. To facilitate an improved position, a 20-inch resistance band is placed below the knees to involve the hip abductors.

As this is a cable-column exercise, three sets of 10 can be done and the weight increased in week 2, or you can use a set weight and an 8-10-12 progression.

Figure 8.29 Cable column standing chop.

Cable Column Standing Lift

The lift is the opposite of the chop. To do the lift, the cable column is placed in its lowest position. Grab the special handle with the hands 12 to 14 inches apart. The action is again pull-push, but you pull one hand to the shoulder and then press the opposite hand overhead while keeping the pulling hand at shoulder height. Press to a position directly over the head (see figure 8.30). Watch for shifting of the hips. Both of these lifts should be done with no more than 20 to 30 pounds at first.

Three sets of 10 can be done and the weight increased in week 2, or you can use a set weight and an 8-10-12 progression.

Figure 8.30 Cable column standing lift.

Kneeling Balance Series

Although this series of exercises develops balance and proprioception, they are also stabilization exercises and so are included in torso workouts. One of the benefits of the kneeling balance series is how these movements link the groin muscles with the torso stabilizers. These exercises are both fun and challenging and can progress into games of catch. At no point do they progress to standing exercises; the risks of falling from a standing position on a stability ball far outweigh the potential benefits. The progression is from two knees on the ball to one knee and eventually to one knee and one foot (see figure 8.31).

Figure 8.31 Kneeling balance series.

Rotational Torso Exercises

Rotational exercises can be divided into three categories: simple rotation, extension or flexion with rotation, and explosive rotation. Standing rotational torso work is the essence of torso training and is done with the medicine ball. We often combine straight-line medicine-ball throwing, explosive extension-oriented medicine-ball work, and rotational throws on the same day. This yields a total-torso workout that is unmatched. My philosophy and current program of medicine-ball training has been heavily influenced by Mark Verstegen of Athletes' Performance Institute in Tempe, Arizona.

Simple Rotation

This book does not cover basic rotational exercise such as twisting and crunches. Simple rotation is defined as single-plane, prone rotation.

Lying Trunk Twist

The lying trunk twist falls in the simple rotation category due to its single-plane nature. Lie on your back with the arms extended at right angles to the body and a stability ball grasped between the legs (see figure 8.32). The legs are held at 90 degrees to the body and are rotated from side to side. The stability ball serves two purposes:

1. The ball engages the adductor muscles, making the exercise serve as a tie-in to the pubic symphysis.
2. The ball actually makes the exercise easier by decreasing the necessary range of motion.

Progress by removing the ball, switching to a smaller ball, or using a heavier ball.

Follow the body-weight progression of 10, 12, then 14 reps on each side over a three-week period.

Figure 8.32 Lying trunk twist.

Russian Twist With Ball

Level 2 The Russian twist is a simple exercise that combines stabilization with rotation. This is a stability-ball variation of the standard Russian twist. The shoulders are kept on the ball with the feet on the floor. The action is to roll on the ball from the tip of the right shoulder to the tip of the left shoulder (see figure 8.33).

Beginners can start with the hands clasped and can progress to a two- to five-kilogram medicine ball. Then follow the body-weight progression or increase the medicine-ball weight.

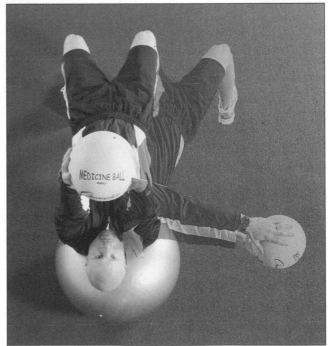

Figure 8.33 Russian twist with ball.

Standing Bodyblade®

Level 3

The standing Bodyblade is an interesting exercise that I have included in the rotational category, although it might fall into the category of "vibrational stabilization." The purpose of the standing Bodyblade is to activate the multifidus, which, along with the transversus abdominis, is a main stabilizer of the lumbar spine. The multifidus muscles lie below the spinal erector group and connect and stabilize the vertebrae, particularly during rotation. To do this exercise, attempt to develop a rhythm with the Bodyblade by oscillating the trunk without moving the hips (see figure 8.34). Unlike the other rotational exercises, the standing Bodyblade is measured in time, not reps. Sets of 30 seconds are generally used once you have learned the movement. Don't be discouraged if you cannot master the oscillation right away. The shorter, less expensive Bodyblade can be used in this exercise.

Figure 8.34   Standing Bodyblade.

Diagonal Plate Raise

Level 2 The diagonal plate raise is an excellent progression to or substitute for the standing lift. This is an extension-rotation movement. The diagonal plate raise is a simple way to address extension-rotation without the use of a pulley system. Move from a squatting position with the plate held outside the left leg to a fully extended position with the plate pressed toward the ceiling (see figure 8.35). It helps to actually look through the hole in the plate. Rotate the hips while pushing off the left leg for a triple extension of the ankle, knee, and hip.

Begin with a 10-kilogram plate, and follow the body-weight progression.

Figure 8.35 Diagonal plate raise.

Medicine-Ball Training

The medicine ball can be used for a number of different outcomes. The medicine ball is an excellent tool for rotator cuff deceleration training, upper-body power, total-body power, and rotational power in the torso. Many of the medicine-ball drills presented here can be viewed as multipurpose. The medicine ball is the key tool in developing a powerful and functional torso. Medicine-ball training can be viewed as Olympic lifting or plyometrics for the torso. None of the torso exercises previously described in this book address velocity, only specific functions such as stabilization or rotation. Medicine-ball training converts all the strength and stability developed in conventional abdominal training to power. The proper medicine-ball progressions develop explosive power in both flexion and rotation safely and effectively. Credit for many of these ideas should go to Mark Verstegen of Athletes' Performance Institute, who has heavily influenced my thinking on the subject of medicine-ball training.

One of the keys to medicine-ball training is proper ball selection (see table 8.1). Most strength athletes believe that heavier is better. With the medicine ball, this is certainly not the case. The key to medicine-ball training is velocity. Any time an athlete struggles to throw the medicine ball, the ball is too heavy. The guidelines for medicine-ball weight in table 8.1 are based on my experience with thousands of athletes. For beginners a lighter ball works better. If you have any doubts about ball weight, go down one kilogram. Emphasis should be on speed of movement, not ball weight. Please remember that these are just guidelines, not absolute requirements. Always remember this simple rule: If it looks too heavy, it probably is.

table 8.1

GUIDELINES FOR MEDICINE-BALL SELECTION

Athlete's weight	Ball weight (rotation)	Ball weight (overhead)
100–135 lb	1 kg	1 kg
135–175 lb	2 kg	2 kg
175–200 lb	3 kg	2 kg
200–250 lb	4 kg	3 kg

Medicine-ball training is far superior when done against a wall. A partner is a poor substitute and negates the plyometric (eccentric to concentric switching) effect of working off a wall. Masonry wall space is highly desirable in a medicine-ball program. A good set of throws should look like a good series of shots or swings and should be fluid, with smooth switching from eccentric to concentric action. Athletes should stand approximately a body-length away from the wall and throw as if they want to damage the wall and the ball. They should throw the ball so that the rebound returns the ball to their hands. Athletes can move closer to or farther from the wall, depending on their power output.

Rotational Throws

Rotational throws are the first technique for developing power in the torso muscles. These exercises are particularly good for hockey, golf, tennis, baseball, and any other sport that requires explosive torso rotation. Athletes should use a sport-specific stance for medicine-ball throwing. Tennis players should look like tennis players when throwing, and hockey players should look like hockey players. Progress throws every three weeks in conjunction with strength-training phases.

Front Twist Throw

The front twist throw (figure 8.36) is a great general rotational exercise for the torso and an excellent way to begin a medicine-ball program. Front twist throws are performed one side at a time. Throw from the hips and feet and then through the trunk. Throw from the ground up with the hands as the final point. Face the wall in a basic defensive stance with the knees bent and the hips down and back, in a fundamental sports-general stance. This is a simple starting point for any athlete.

Perform 10 throws on the right side, then 10 throws on the left. Do three sets of 10 throws on each side for three weeks. Don't attempt to increase volume; throw harder and throw better. This is the progression for all rotational medicine-ball work to follow.

Figure 8.36 Front twist throw.

Alternating Front Twist Throw

The alternating front twist throw is the same as the front twist throw, but you alternate sides for 20 throws, instead of performing 10 throws from one side and then 10 from the other. The movement should look fluid and athletic as you move from side to side. This exercise demands slightly more coordination and athleticism.

Side Throw

The side throw imitates a number of sports. This drill develops explosive rotational torso strength for tennis, field hockey, hockey, lacrosse, and baseball. In the side throw (figure 8.37), the emphasis should be on throwing with the hips and initiating the action from the back foot. A good throw should look like a good swing or a good shot. Develop a throwing style that has the appearance of the skill that you are trying to improve. For a hockey player, for instance, the side throw should look like a slap shot; for a baseball player, it should look like a good swing.

Figure 8.37 Side throw.

Side Twist Throw With Step

The next step in the progression is to add movement to the throw. In level 4, step toward the wall with the front foot to increase the force being generated from the back foot. Emphasis is on shifting weight from the front foot to the back foot. All other aspects of the side throw remain the same.

Back Twist Throw

The back twist throw is by far the most difficult to execute and can be tough on a beginner's back. Do not perform this exercise without mastering the first four levels. To do the back twist throw, stand with the back toward the wall and the feet pointing straight ahead. Then throw the ball over the shoulder to the wall (figure 8.38). Initially you may throw at waist height or slightly higher until you develop the flexibility necessary to throw at shoulder height or higher.

Figure 8.38   Back twist throw.

Single-Leg Front Twist Throw

This advanced exercise adds difficulty as well as great proprioceptive stimulus for the ankle, knee, and hip. It requires a higher level of balance and coordination and heavily involves the hip rotator musculature of the stance leg. Execute the front twist throw described earlier from a single-leg stance. If you are throwing from the left side, stand on the right foot, as shown in figure 8.39. The throw begins with the right foot off the ground and forward of the body, and the ball back behind the hip. As the throw is executed, the hips rotate, the arms come forward, and the leg moves back. This will eventually become a smooth, coordinated movement.

Figure 8.39 Single-leg front twist throw.

Overhead Throws

Overhead throws target the rectus abdominis group and also provide training for the rotator cuff. Do three sets of 10 to 20 reps for overhead throws.

Standing Overhead Throw

The standing overhead throw (figure 8.40) is the starting point for all overhead throwing variations. The drill is similar to a soccer throw-in, but with the feet shoulder-width apart and not staggered. Use the trunk more than the arms to throw the ball. This is an excellent drill for any throwing athlete.

Do three sets of 10 reps. I do not recommend single-arm throws because the stress of catching with a single arm is too great for the shoulder.

Figure 8.40 Standing overhead throw.

Standing Overhead Throw With Stagger

The standing overhead throw can be done from a staggered stance to provide greater leg involvement, increased velocity, and trunk involvement. Do not progress to the staggered standing overhead until the skill of throwing with the torso has been mastered.

Do three sets of 10 with the right foot in front and then 10 with the left foot in front.

Standing Overhead With Step

This throw is the same as the standing overhead throw in a staggered stance, except now you step into the throw.

Standing Chop

The standing chop combines overhead throwing with flexion and rotation. The ball is taken over one shoulder in both hands and then chopped down at the wall.

For all overhead throws, beginners should use the following sequence two times per week:

Week 1: 1 3 10. Don't throw all out.

Week 2: 2 3 10. Increase effort of throws. Additional 2 3 10 twist pass on your backhand for baseball, golf, hockey, and tennis.

Week 3: 3 3 10. Additional 2 3 10 twist pass on your backhand.

Try to make this a fast-paced workout, whether with a partner or against the wall. In the first three weeks, gradually build up the effort. Try wearing a heart rate monitor and try to keep the heart rate up.

Torso work is an area of functional training that is changing significantly. It is clearly not enough to do a few sit-ups after the workout. Research shows that torso strength aids in the development of speed and power and reduces injuries. A well-designed torso program has a positive influence on all areas of performance. Design your torso program to develop strength and power in all planes and at varying speeds. Stabilization and rotation are key skills for performance enhancement and injury reduction.

BALANCED UPPER-BODY STRENGTH AND STABILITY

Many books and articles have been published that detail how to do various upper-body strength exercises. In spite of all the advice to the contrary, athletes still overemphasize the development of the "mirror muscles" in the chest and arms that contribute to a muscular appearance. The purpose of this chapter is to reinforce a balance between pressing and pulling and to introduce new concepts in using chin-ups, rows, and variations to prevent shoulder injury.

Functional upper-body exercise is divided primarily into pushing and pulling. Other single-joint movements are not truly functional and work muscles only in isolation. Although single-joint movements may be necessary in corrective or stabilization exercises, the key to functional upper-body training is the balance between pushing and pulling.

Pulling for Injury Prevention

In most strength training programs, pulling movements such as chin-ups and rows are given little if any emphasis. Although many articles written over the last 50 years on upper-back development have cited pull-ups and chin-ups as keys to back development, most athletes ignore these exercises for one simple reason: Pull-ups and chin-ups are just too hard. Most athletes instead perform lat pull-downs for the muscles of the upper back under the mistaken assumption that this is all that is necessary, and many completely ignore rowing movements. This type of unbalanced program often leads to overdevelopment of the pressing muscles, postural problems, and shoulder injury.

An essential goal of a sound upper-body program is to equally emphasize all the major upper-body movement patterns. Unfortunately, few athletes think they look better because they have excellent back development. The emphasis is usually chest, chest, and more chest. This is an unfortunate by-product of the muscle magazine education that many trainees and trainers have received.

A functional upper-body program should include a proportional number of sets of horizontal pulling (rowing), vertical pulling (chin-up), overhead pressing, and supine pressing exercises. In simple terms, there should be a set of pulling exercise for every set of pushing exercise. In the vast majority of strength programs, this is not the case. They generally offer lots of pressing and very little pulling.

This type of program can lead to postural problems because of the overdevelopment of the pectorals and underdevelopment of the scapula (shoulder blade) retractors. More important, a program that does not provide an equal number of pulling and pushing movements predisposes athletes to overuse shoulder injuries, especially rotator cuff tendinitis. The incidence of rotator cuff tendinitis among athletes who do a lot of bench-pressing is extremely high. In my opinion, this is not due to the bench press itself but rather to the lack of appropriate pulling movements. It is extremely important that athletes possess an appropriate ratio of pulling strength to pushing strength. This is best estimated by comparing an athlete's maximum number of pull-ups to his or her maximum bench press weight. Consideration must be given to body weight, but athletes capable of bench-pressing well over their body weight should also be capable of pulling their body weight, regardless of size. For example, a 200-pound athlete who can bench-press 300 pounds should be able to perform 12 to 15 chin-ups. A 300-pound athlete who can bench-press 400 pounds should be able to do 5 to 8 chin-ups (see table 9.1).

table 9.1

MAXIMUM CHIN-UPS OF SELECTED GROUPS (ELBOWS TO FULL EXTENSION)

Elite male (National Hockey League)	20–30
NFL lineman (320 pounds)	7+
NFL skill position	15–20
College male (Division 1)	20–30
Elite female (Olympic gold medalist, 152 pounds)	15
College female (Division 1 field hockey)	10+

These numbers are not averages, but examples from top performers. These numbers are provided merely to indicate what is possible in a program with proper design and proper emphasis.

A properly designed strength program includes at least three sets each of two chin-up variations per week as well as a minimum of three sets of two rowing movements per week. See table 9.2. An important principle in program design is to use numerous variations of the same type of movement. Either the specific type of vertical and horizontal pull should change every three weeks, or the number of repetitions should change every three weeks; in some cases, both should change.

table 9.2

SAMPLE HORIZONTAL AND VERTICAL PULL VARIATIONS

Phase 1			
Day 1	Chin-up		3×8
	Dumbbell row		3×8
Day 2	Parallel-grip pull-up		3×8
	Inverted row		3×8
Phase 2			
Day 1	Pull-up		$3 \times 3, 1 \times 10$
	One-arm, one-leg row		3×8 with each arm
Day 2	Alternate-grip chin-up		4×3
	Upper-back dumbbell row		3×5

Vertical Pulling Movements

Variation is the key to continued strength gain. Vary the type of exercise and the loading pattern every three weeks.

Chin-Up

The chin-up is the easiest of the upper-body pulling movements due to the supinated grip (palms facing in toward the body) and corresponding gain in biceps assistance. Use a 12- to 14-inch grip width. Essential techniques for all the vertical pulling movements are to fully extend the elbows and to allow the scapula to elevate. Athletes should not be allowed to cheat at all. Over the first eight weeks, don't be too concerned with variety. Beginners need less variety than advanced trainees.

Chin-ups and the variations are cycled in the strength program to correspond with the other major exercises (hang clean, front squat, bench press). Do three sets of 10 chin-ups, three to five sets of 5, and three to five sets of 3.

Although machines are available to assist with chin-ups and pull-ups, a much simpler system can be set up for far less money. Simply loop a heavy-duty resistance band (such as the ones made by JumpStretch, which are well constructed and come in heavy, medium, and light resistances) over the pull-up bar. Place one knee in the band, and lower to the start position (figure 9.1). The elastic energy of the band assists you in the ascent. You can work down progressively from heavy- to light-resistance bands and then to unassisted full body weight. Once you can perform one unassisted chin-up, you can use the eight-week program in table 9.3. It is not unusual for athletes to advance from one chin-up to five after this eight-week progression.

Athletes who can perform more than 10 chin-ups should use a dip belt to add additional weight. Cycle the vertical pulling movements as you do the core lifts. When the program calls for three reps, increase the weight drastically and perform sets of three reps. It is not unusual for our male athletes to use 90 or more pounds for sets of three and for our female athletes to use in excess of 25 pounds.

A healthy athlete who can perform five assisted chin-ups with a heavy band should never do pull-downs. Only extremely overweight athletes who have a poor strength–to–body weight ratio should perform pull-downs. There is no rationale for pull-downs by healthy athletes who are capable of chin-ups or assisted chin-ups. Pull-downs are simply an easy way out for people who do not want to do chin-ups.

Figure 9.1 Assisted chin-up.

table 9.3

EIGHT-WEEK CHIN-UP PROGRESSION

This program is intended to be done two times per week only.

Week 1	4 × 1 (This means four single reps, with a 3- to 5-second eccentric contraction at the end of the last rep.)
Week 2	1 × 2, 3 × 1
Week 3	2 × 2, 2 × 1
Week 4	3 × 2, 1 × 1
Week 5	4 × 2
Week 6	1 × 3, 3 × 2
Week 7	2 × 3, 2 × 2
Week 8	3 × 3, 1 × 2

Parallel-Grip Pull-Up

This excellent upper-body pulling exercise is similar to the chin-up but targets the forearm flexors (brachialis and brachioradialis) due to the neutral hand position. Parallel-grip pull-ups can be done on a pull-up bar equipped with a V handle or parallel handles (see figure 9.2). Execution is the same as for the chin-up; only the hand position differs.

Figure 9.2 Parallel-grip pull-up.

Pull-Up

The pull-up is a more difficult exercise than the chin-up or parallel-grip pull-up. In the pull-up the hands are pronated (palms forward). There is less assistance from the muscles of the upper arm and correspondingly more stress on the back muscles, which significantly increases the difficulty. The pull-up should be the third exercise done in the upper-body program, after a minimum of three weeks of chin-ups and parallel-grip pull-ups.

Alternate-Grip Pull-Up

The alternate-grip pull-up is an excellent variation for sports such as hockey, baseball, and lacrosse that use an alternate grip. The number of sets must always be an even number to allow an equal number of overhand and underhand sets.

Sternum Chin-Up

The sternum chin-up is a difficult variation for even advanced athletes. To do the sternum chin-up, pull the sternum up to the bar rather than pull the chin above the bar (see figure 9.3). This requires using the scapula retractors to a greater degree and increases their range of motion by three to four inches.

Figure 9.3   Sternum chin-up.

Horizontal Pulling Movements

Horizontal pulling movements, or rowing movements, are important for two reasons:

1. Rows help prevent injury.
2. Rows are a true antagonistic movement to the bench press. Although chin-ups and their variations are important, rowing movements target both the muscles and the movement patterns that directly oppose those trained with the bench press.

Despite their importance, rows are frequently omitted from strength programs.

Rowing motions are an area of functional training that is undergoing great change. Recent advances in athletic training and physical therapy have illustrated that the body is linked posteriorly in a diagonal pattern. Force is transmitted from the ground through the leg to the hip and then across the SI joint (sacro-iliac joint) into the opposite latissimus dorsi (the lat, a surface back muscle) and shoulder complex. The keys in this system of cross-linkage are the gluteus medius and quadratus lumborum, which stabilize the pelvis, and the hip rotator group, which stabilizes the hip. The hip rotator group is of particular importance because all force transferred from the ground must move through a stable hip to properly transfer to the upper body. Until very recently, this vital group has been effectively ignored. The hip rotators are the "rotator cuff" of the lower body but do not get the respect and attention that the shoulder rotator cuff muscles of the upper body get. All force originating at the ground, whether a golf swing or a home run, must transfer through a strong, flexible, and stable hip rotator group. The hip rotators must be given particular attention in program design. Rowing movements with a cable column help strengthen this undertrained area.

Dumbbell Row

The dumbbell row is the simplest of rowing movements and can help beginners learn proper back position. Begin in a wide squat stance with the knees out over the feet. Then lean forward and place one hand on a bench to stabilize your torso and take stress off the low back. The back is slightly arched, and the abdominals are drawn in. Concentrate first on moving the scapula and then the elbow to bring the dumbbell back to the hip (figure 9.4). This movement is great for beginners but does not work the hip rotator group due to the double-leg stance.

Do three sets of 5 to 10 reps, depending on the training phase.

Figure 9.4 Dumbbell row.

Inverted Row

The inverted row can be described as a pull-up or chin-up for the scapula retractors. This is a wonderfully simple yet challenging movement that teaches torso stabilization and develops strength in the scapula retractors and rear deltoid. Although the movement appears simple, the inverted row is a humbling exercise for even the strongest athletes. Athletes with strong pressing muscles will be unpleasantly surprised at how few quality inverted rows they can perform.

To perform the inverted row, place a bar in a power rack in the bench press position (waist height). A bench is placed approximately three quarters of a body length away. Put the feet on the bench and the hands on the bar, and hold the torso perfectly straight. The toes are pointed up, and the feet are together. From this position, simply pull the chest to the bar (see figure 9.5). Most athletes are unable to touch the chest to the bar after the first rep, due to weakness in the scapula retractors and posterior deltoid. This exercise stresses not only the upper back but also the entire torso. To increase the functional overload of the torso muscles, advanced athletes can perform this exercise with the feet on a stability ball instead of a bench. The unstable support causes the trunk and shoulder stabilizers to work harder.

The number of reps varies by strength level. Beginners who cannot perform the movement correctly should not use it, because various adaptations for beginners, such as putting the feet on the floor instead of a bench, show limited success.

Figure 9.5 Inverted row.

One-Arm, One-Leg Row (Static Hips)

Level 1

The one-arm, one-leg row is the first exercise in the rowing progression to address the hip rotators as stabilizers. Either a low pulley setup or an adjustable cable column is needed. Young athletes can do this exercise with any tubing apparatus with a handle, but larger or stronger athletes quickly adapt to the elastic resistance. To do the one-arm, one-leg row, stand on one foot to execute a row with the opposite hand (see figure 9.6). In the single-leg stance, the row is not only an upper-back exercise but a stabilization exercise for the ankle, knee, and hip. The one-leg stance elevates the row to a complex exercise that develops stability, proprioception, and strength. The one-arm, one-leg row should initially emphasize stabilization. Attempt to stabilize the ankle, knee, and hip while rowing to a position just below the pectoral muscle of the chest. In all cable rowing movements, shoulder rotator cuff work can be added by beginning with the upper arm internally rotated and finishing with the hand in a neutral position. The rotator cuff becomes involved in the row as the shoulder position changes.

Do three sets of 5 to 10 reps, depending on training phase.

Figure 9.6 One-arm, one-leg row (static hips).

One-Arm, One-Leg Row (Dynamic)

Level 2 The only difference between the dynamic and static versions of this exercise is that the athlete is allowed to reach into the cable column in the dynamic version. The reach involves trunk rotation and hip internal rotation, and a load is placed on the hip lateral (external) rotators as the rowing movement is completed. This movement dynamically stresses the body from ankle to shoulder. In a sense, the athlete is allowed to "cheat" by increasing hip movement.

Do three sets of 5 to 10 reps, depending on training phase.

One-Arm, Two-Leg Rotational Row

The one-arm, two-leg rotational row is borrowed from performance enhancement expert Mark Verstegen. It is an extremely dynamic movement that incorporates leg extension, hip internal rotation, and trunk rotation into a total-body rowing exercise. This functional and integrated exercise is best described as half squat, half row. I believe this relatively new exercise will soon be a staple in all functional training programs. Assume a position with the shoulders aligned with the line of pull of a cable column or low pulley. Reach across the body to grasp the handle, and pull the handle to the hip while standing up tall (figure 9.7). You use the squatting muscles in conjunction with the rowing muscles to simultaneously extend the legs, rotate the trunk, and extend the shoulder. The only muscles not stressed by this exercise are the pressing muscles. This exercise mimics the action used in changes of direction. Try to visualize the forces needed to brake and change direction and the exercise will take on whole new relevance.

Do three sets of 5 to 10 reps, depending on training phase.

Figure 9.7 One-arm, two-leg rotational row.

Squat and Pull

The squat and pull (figure 9.8) combines a double-leg squatting action with a one-arm row. This exercise is also done using the cable column. You can use more weight in this exercise due to the assistance of the legs and the trunk rotators. This movement is good for in-season work, when saving time with combination movements is desirable.

Do three sets of 5 to 10 reps, depending on training phase.

Figure 9.8 Squat and pull.

One-Leg Squat and Pull

The one-leg squat and pull and the one-arm, two-leg rotational row are the most difficult and most functional of the rowing movements. The one-leg squat and pull combines the dynamic movement of the one-arm, one-leg row and the lower-body demand of the one-leg squat. The exercise works the upper-back musculature while also developing single-leg strength, balance, and stability. In the one-leg squat and pull, almost touch the knee of the free leg to the ground when returning the weight to the starting position (see figure 9.9).

Do three sets of 5 to 10 reps, depending on training phase.

Figure 9.9 One-leg squat and pull.

Upper-Body Pressing Exercises

This section focuses on functional upper-body strength rather than the bench press. Athletes that I train perform bench presses, dumbbell bench presses, and numerous other variations of supine pressing movements. I am not against the bench press, but my philosophy is balanced training in which performance in one relatively unimportant lift is not overemphasized. In functional training it is important that the combination of supine and overhead pressing should not take up more than 30 minutes twice per week. Any additional time spent on pressing movements detracts from the training of other muscle groups and disturbs the balance of the program.

Table 9.4 presents a set of general guidelines that are helpful in program design and strength evaluation. The guidelines are provided to help coaches, trainers, and athletes achieve greater balance among the different supine pressing exercises. You can improve your bench press numbers by increasing other related lifts. Often athletes are so focused on one lift that they actually retard their progress. Strive for balanced pressing strength in which strength is developed at a variety of angles (incline, overhead) along with stability (by using dumbbells). One angle or one action should not become dominant. All upper-body dumbbell work is prescribed with these guidelines

table 9.4

PROPER STRENGTH RELATIONSHIP IN UPPER-BODY PRESSES

This chart shows the amount of weight that an athlete should be able to lift after a proper training program to develop balanced upper-body pressing strength.

Bench press Example: 300 lb max	Incline bench 240 lb (80% of bench press max)	Dumbbell bench press 95 × 5 (64% of bench max/2 to get dumbbell weight)	Dumbbell incline 77 × 5 (80% of dumbbell bench)
250	200	80 × 5	65 × 5
200	160	65 × 5	50 × 5
150	120	48 × 5	40 × 5

in mind. Beginners need to increase weights slowly to develop the necessary balance and stability to lift heavier weights.

Push-Ups

The push-up is one of the most underrated exercises in the upper-body program. Push-ups are upper-body pressing movements that require no equipment and offer almost limitless variations. The push-up is an excellent exercise for larger athletes who need to improve their strength–to–body weight ratios. For this reason alone push-ups are a great exercise in football training programs. Another great advantage of the push-up is that it combines upper-body training with torso development. Many larger athletes or athletes who are weak throughout the torso have difficulty maintaining the proper body position for a push-up. In addition, push-ups work the shoulder blade area in a way that the bench press cannot.

Feet-Elevated Push-Up

The feet-elevated push-up (figure 9.10) is the simplest way to increase the difficulty of the push-up. Athletes who find the push up easy can elevate the feet from 12 to 24 inches to increase the difficulty without adding any external resistance.

Figure 9.10 Feet-elevated push-up.

Core Board Rotational Push-Up

This exercise uses the Reebok Core Board, a useful tool in any functional training program. The Core Board rotational push-up can be done only with a Reebok Core Board, which allows the athlete to work in two planes of movement simultaneously (see figure 9.11). The Core Board rotational push-up utilizes the rotational capabilities of the board to work the muscles of the upper back along with the chest muscles, shoulder muscles, and triceps, which are worked in a normal push-up.

Figure 9.11   Core Board rotational push-up.

Dumbbell Rotational Push-Up

To do the dumbbell rotational push-up, first perform a push-up with dumbbells grasped in the hands. Finish the push-up by balancing on one hand and lifting the other hand into a side-support position: on one hand, the shoulders and arms aligned in a plane perpendicular to the floor (figure 9.12). This pressing exercise develops upper-body strength, torso strength, and shoulder stability, so it offers great bang for the buck when training time is limited.

Figure 9.12   Dumbbell rotational push-up.

Stability-Ball Push-Up

The stability-ball push-up (figure 9.13) can be done in a feet-elevated version or with a weight vest. It develops proprioception in the upper body and the torso and places the hands in a much more sports-general position. The hand position in the stability-ball push-up is very similar to the specific hand position used by football linemen.

Do three sets of 5 to 10 reps, depending on training phase. More push-up reps can be done in endurance phases.

Figure 9.13 Stability-ball push-up.

The proper progression for push-ups is illustrated in figure 9.14.

Scapulothoracic Functional Training

Some exercises that initially appear nonfunctional may in fact be useful and improve function at certain joints. The scapulothoracic (shoulder blade–rib cage) joint is one of three areas that need short-range isolating exercise to improve their function and at the same time the function of the entire shoulder joint. The mistake in shoulder training has been to approach it as an either/or proposition. Coaches tend to view training for the shoulder musculature either as multijoint training and thus emphasize overhead pressing or as single-joint training and thus emphasize glenohumeral (shoulder socket–upper arm) exercises such as front, side and "empty can" dumbbell raises. The best approach is to combine overhead presses for strength with exercises to improve scapulothoracic stability for injury prevention. Standing lateral raises and similar exercises work the deltoid muscles in a nonfunctional manner and do not necessarily contribute to the stability of the scapula. The target of shoulder circuit or shoulder "prehabilitation" exercises should be movement and stabilization of the scapula, not movement of the humerus (upper arm bone). For this reason these exercises need to be done prone. Standing shoulder flexion exercises, such as lateral raises and empty can exercises, do not properly target

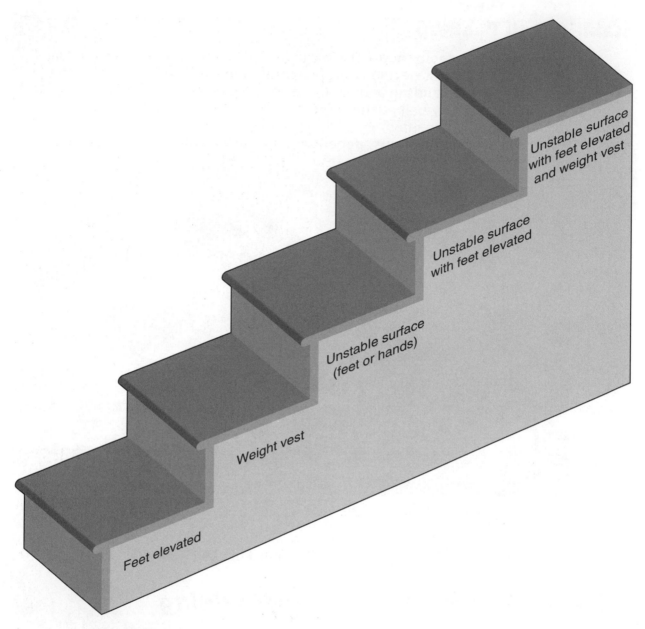

Figure 9.14 Push-up progression.

the scapulothoracic joint. The function of the scapulothoracic joint is critical for injury reduction. Strengthening the rotator cuff muscles without strengthening the scapula stabilizers does only half the job. Even a strong rotator cuff needs a stable base from which to operate. This stable base is provided by the scapulothoracic joint.

Prone Shoulder Circuit

The letters Y, T, W, and L are used to describe the prone positions in which to perform scapula retraction or elevation movements. (This scheme is from Sue Falsone of Athletes' Performance Institute in Tempe, Arizona.) The shape of the letter suggests the placement of the arms in relation to the body. See figure 9.15.

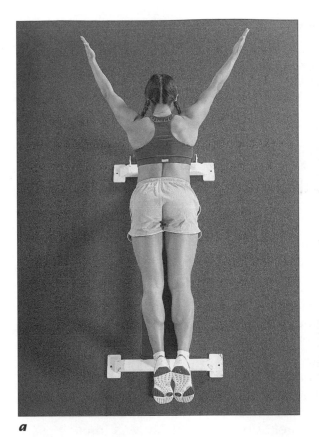

a

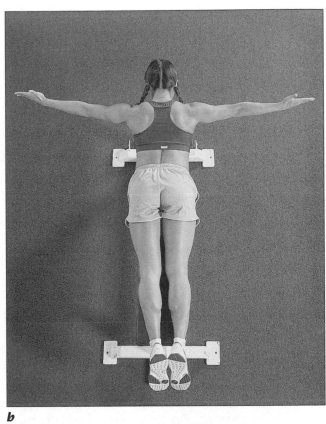

b

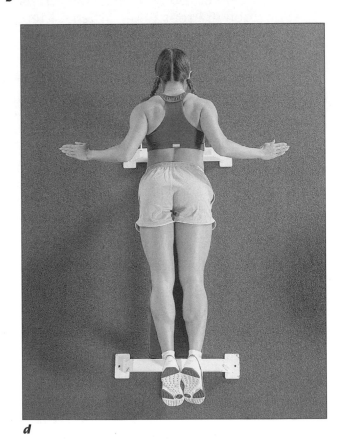

c   d

Figure 9.15 Prone shoulder circuit.

Y = Arms from 45 to 90 degrees above shoulder level, with the thumbs pointed up to facilitate external rotation.

T = With the upper arm at a 90-degree angle to the torso and the thumbs pointed up. The key to this position is to retract the scapula and maintain a 90-degree angle at the shoulder. Many athletes with weak scapula retractors pull the arms down to the sides slightly to substitute action of the lats for that of the scapula retractors. This produces an adduction movement instead of a retraction movement and should be guarded against carefully. The angle should never be less than 90 degrees, which indicates lat substitution.

W = Upper arm at a 45-degree angle to the torso, elbow flexed 90 degrees. Think of this as a kind of reverse pec deck movement. Emphasize scapula retraction.

L = Upper arm as close to the side as possible, elbow flexed 90 degrees. This combines retraction and external rotation.

The circuit is simple and probably somewhat familiar to many physical therapists and athletic trainers, but the key is in how the athlete thinks about the execution of the movements. The athlete must move the arms by *moving the scapulothoracic joint,* not the reverse. The initial emphasis is on scapulo-thoracic movement, not glenohumeral movement. This approach changes the exercises from deltoid exercises to scapula-stabilizing exercises.

Begin with eight reps in each position *with no weight* and without resting between exercises. These must be done in the order Y-T-W-L, for a total of 32 reps per set. Do two sets. Add 2 reps per week, up to sets of 16 reps in each position (64 reps total). When 64 reps can be done, go back to sets of 8 with one- to two-pound dumbbells.

The upper body may be the most difficult area to functionally train because of a fascination with training it for appearance. Athletes may be reluctant to perform push-ups instead of bench presses or to work on back muscles that they cannot see. Experimenting with the chin-up and push-up variations can be valuable. Athletes may find that they do not have the torso stability and strength to perform the inverted row or the stability ball push-up and thus come to understand and appreciate functional training for the upper body. Don't fight to remove sacred cows like the bench press; simply incorporate more functional exercise into the program. A slow transition can help overcome resistance to functional training in this difficult area.

10

PLYOMETRIC TRAINING FOR POWER AND INJURY PREVENTION

Training for power is one of the most controversial topics in athletic training. Most athletes would love to be more powerful, but few agree on the methodology. Plyometrics, medicine-ball throws (chapter 8), and Olympic lifts (chapter 11) are all effective methods to develop power output. Each method has its proponents and opponents. Your likes, dislikes, and areas of expertise determine the method you use. The line between safe technique and functional training can often become blurred. What some experts deem functional is not always safe when performed under load. Athletes, coaches, and trainers need to decide whether they are comfortable teaching fast movements in flexed postures with weights, as some coaches are currently recommending, or whether power development should come through a slightly more conventional combination of Olympic lifts, plyometrics, and medicine-ball work, which is the approach used at our training facility. A combination of Olympic lifting, medicine-ball throws, and plyometrics is the best way to develop explosive power, and this can be accomplished safely if certain guidelines are followed. This chapter describes plyometric training.

Like many current issues in functional training, plyometric training can be controversial. Many experts caution against the initiation of a plyometric program for athletes who do not have the proper leg strength. Articles on plyometric training often suggest that an athlete needs to squat a weight equal to two times his or her body weight prior to even commencing a plyometric program. This is a ridiculous guideline that eliminates nearly 90 percent of the athletes who have ever trained at our facility. The two-times-body-weight guideline was actually suggested years ago as a guideline to begin high-level plyometrics but somewhere along the line was incorrectly applied to all plyometric training. Other authors suggest an eight-week strength phase before commencing a plyometric program. Although this suggestion is slightly more rational, it is still not practical because most athletes train for only 10 to 12 weeks in the off-season. An eight-week strength phase leaves only four weeks of plyometric training at most, a period far too short in which to implement a periodized program.

The keys to a plyometric program are that the exercises are taught in a progressive manner and that progress is based on competence, not a predetermined timeline. If an athlete cannot move beyond phase 1 skills, that athlete should stay in phase 1 for an additional two or three weeks before attempting to progress. Don't try to force adaptation.

The Progressive Plyometric Program

The progressive plyometric program is actually a program that teaches jumping and landing skills before introducing what many coaches and athletes would recognize as plyometrics. The strength of this type of program is that it initially puts injury prevention before power development.

Phases 1 through 3 of this progressive plyometric program are not "true" plyometrics. Phases 1 through 3 consist of drills to teach jumping skills, to develop landing with great stability, and to introduce the elastic component of jumping. This progressive plyometric program does not introduce true plyometrics until phase 4.

What are "true" plyometrics? True plyometric drills require the athlete to reduce the time spent on the ground. The athlete learns to minimize the amortization (shock absorption) phase and to respond aggressively to the ground. Although the science behind plyometric training is sound, we have done a poor job of facing the realities and disparities of the human body. We must crawl before we walk and walk before we run. The same applies to plyometrics. We must learn to jump off the ground and properly land on the ground before we attempt to minimize time spent on the ground. Gravity is the enemy of the large athlete, the young athlete, and the weak athlete, and gravity must be respected when teaching an athlete to jump or when attempting to develop explosive power.

Plyometric drills for each phase are classified as linear drills or lateral drills. The volume of a plyometric program is based on number of foot contacts. We keep the number of foot contacts low and gradually increase the intensity of the jumps. Intensity is increased by either increasing the contribution of gravity or by attempting to change the nature of the amortization phase. This is accomplished either by jumping over an object rather than up on an object or by introducing an elastic component through a "bounce" and then a rebound. Generally athletes do not exceed 150 foot contacts per week, even in the later phases. What changes is the intensity of the jumps, not the volume.

Phase 1: Single Response, Stabilization

In this progressive plyometric program, the emphasis of the first phase is on learning to jump and land. Athletes should be taught to summate forces using the arms and hips and to *land softly*. The more softly the athlete lands, the better. Athletes must learn to absorb force with the muscles, not with the joints.

The purpose of phase 1 is to develop eccentric strength. This is the most important and unfortunately the most overlooked phase of plyometric training. Skipping or attempting to abbreviate phase 1 is the main cause of injury. Phase 1 generally lasts three to four weeks but should last as long as necessary for each athlete. The key is to develop eccentric strength and stability, and coaches and athletes should take as long as they need to in this phase. No matter what performance level an athlete has achieved, he or she should always begin in phase 1. Whether the athlete is a pro or a middle school student, phase 1 lasts a minimum of three weeks. The goal of phase 1 is to develop the eccentric strength necessary to land. Think of phase 1 as tendon training.

In addition, plyometric drills for each phase will always be broken down into linear drills or lateral drills. In phase 1 athletes perform only one exercise each from the linear and lateral drill categories, and they do three to five sets of five jumps. For lateral jumps, they perform three sets of five landings on each leg.

The following exercises should be done two days per week.

Box Jump

This linear exercise is the most basic of all the jumping drills. Select a box height that is appropriate for your athletic ability. Many athletes want to inflate their egos by using a box that is too high. The coach should not be afraid to choose the box for the athlete if the athlete displays a poor sense of his or her own jumping ability. For beginners, box height ranges from 4 to 24 inches depending on the skill level of the athlete. Talented beginners may begin as high as 30 inches. Do three to five sets of 5 jumps, up to 25 jumps total, or in plyometric lingo, 25 foot contacts.

The criteria for evaluating box height are simple.

1. Can the athlete land quietly?
2. Does the athlete land in the same position that he or she took off in? If the landing squat is deeper than the takeoff squat, the box is too high.

The comparison between landing and take-off is a great suggestion made by Oregon strength coach and plyometrics expert Jim Radcliffe in his lectures and writings. This simple, no-nonsense concept helps coaches determine whether athletes are performing the box jump correctly. The landing position should never be deeper than a half-squat position. See figure 10.1.

Figure 10.1 Box jump.

Single-Leg Box Jump

Use the technique described for the box jump, but begin with a four-inch box. Do three sets of 5 jumps per leg, for a total of 15 jumps per leg. See figure 10.2.

Figure 10.2 Single-leg box jump.

Single-Leg Lateral Box Jump

This lateral phase exercise is also done two days per week. To do the single-leg lateral box jump, jump from the side of a four-inch box to the top of the box (figure 10.3). The key is a stable, quiet landing on one leg.

Do three medial jumps (toward the midline of the body) and three lateral jumps (away from the midline of the body) per leg. The stabilization forces are markedly different in each case. Do three sets of six jumps (three medial and three lateral) per leg.

Figure 10.3 Single-leg lateral box jump.

Phase 2: Multiple Response, Stabilization

In phase 2, gravity becomes a larger component of the drills. Instead of simply jumping up on a box as in phase 1, you now jump over an obstacle (which includes both a vertical and a horizontal component) or move from right foot to left foot in lateral drills. This greatly increases the eccentric load on the muscle. The goal of soft landing remains the same, but the force of gravity greatly increases the eccentric strength needed. Note that progression is done by increasing the eccentric load of the jumps rather than by increasing the number of jumps.

The major difference between the following linear drills and those in phase 1 is the introduction of gravity. Instead of jumping up on a box, the athlete jumps over an object, usually a hurdle from 6 to 30 inches tall, depending on the type of jump and the athlete's skill level.

Hurdle Jump and Stick

The hurdle jump and stick is a jump over a hurdle ranging in height from 12 to 30 inches with a quiet, stable landing (figure 10.4). Small hurdles can be a problem, so use 12-inch hurdles with 6-inch extenders or 24-inch hurdles intended for middle school track and field.

Do three to five sets of five hurdles, for a total of 15 to 25 jumps.

Figure 10.4　Hurdle jump and stick.

One-Leg Hurdle Hop and Stick

Use the technique described for the hurdle hop and stick, only with six-inch hurdles. In the one-leg hurdle hop and stick, you'll jump off of and land on the same leg (see figure 10.5). This drill can be done over sticks or lines if landing stability is an issue.

Do three sets of 5 jumps on each leg, 30 jumps total.

Figure 10.5 One-leg hurdle hop and stick.

Heiden and Stick

Heiden and stick is a basic lateral exercise that is known by numerous names, including skaters or skate hops. Jump from right to left and hold the landing for a full second before jumping back to the opposite side. You should attempt to jump both up and out (see figure 10.6).

Do three sets of 5 jumps on each leg, 30 jumps total.

Figure 10.6   Heiden and stick.

Zigzag Bound and Stick

The zigzag bound and stick adds a linear component to the lateral action of the Heiden. Instead of jumping directly to the side, the push-off is forward at a 45-degree angle (see figure 10.7).

Do three sets of 5 jumps on each leg, 30 total jumps.

Figure 10.7 Zigzag bound and stick.

Phase 3: Multiple Jumps, Introduction of Elastic Component

The third phase begins to approach what many coaches and athletes would consider real plyometrics. The emphasis in phase 3 is on switching from an eccentric contraction to a concentric contraction rather than simply developing eccentric strength. Although eccentric-to-concentric switching is the essence of plyometric training, the root of most plyometrics-related injuries is neglecting the development of eccentric landing skills. Phases 1 and 2 lay the essential groundwork for injury prevention and for later stretch-shortening-cycle work. Phase 3 introduces the stretch-shortening cycle by incorporating a bounce into the drills. The key is to gradually increase the type and amount of stress applied to the muscle and, more importantly, to the connective tissue.

The exercises are basically the same as in phase 2, but they are done with a bounce before doing the next jump. Stretch shortening is introduced without a drastic change in program. Intensity increases, but not volume.

Hurdle Hop With Bounce

Use the same technique as for the hurdle jump and stick (page 150), but replace the stuck landing with a bounce before the next takeoff.

One-Leg Hurdle Hop With Bounce

Use the same technique as for the one-leg hurdle hop and stick (page 151), but replace the stable landing with a bounce before the next takeoff. If athletes struggle with this drill, they should resume phase 2 and stick the landing.

Zigzag Bound With Bounce

Use the same technique as for the zigzag bound in phase 2, but bounce prior to the next takeoff.

Phase 4: Multiple Jumps, Elastic Response

Phase 4 moves into the realm of what most coaches and athletes consider plyometrics. In this phase, the emphasis is on reacting to the ground and minimizing ground contact time. If you are wondering, "What took you so long?" the answer is that our approach is safety and mastery first. The biggest mistake of an approach that is too conservative is that the early phases are extended longer than necessary.

In phase 4 you should minimize time spent on the ground and make an elastic, explosive, but quiet transition from eccentric to concentric contraction. When great athletes perform plyometrics, one thing jumps out. You see a great deal of explosiveness but hear little very little. The nervous system and the muscular system do most of the work, with little stress on the joints. This is the goal of the progressive plyometric program.

Hurdle Jumps

This is a linear drill in which the athlete does double-leg jumps over hurdles.

Power Skip

This is a linear drill in which the athlete adds aggressive hip extension to the warm-up skip to gain both height and distance (see figure 10.8).

Figure 10.8 Power skip.

Lateral Bound

The lateral bound is an aggressive lateral pushoff moving from right to left or left to right (see figure 10.9). The athlete performs aggressive abduction to generate lateral power.

Figure 10.9 Lateral bound.

Crossover Bound

This is a lateral drill in which the power is generated from an aggressive push by the front leg in a crossover step (see figure 10.10).

Figure 10.10 Crossover bound.

Cross-Behind Bound

The cross-behind bound is a lateral drill in which the emphasis is placed on the adductor group as the force producers. Although the drill will look much like the previous drill, the work is not done by the crossover leg but by the leg that is behind. This is an aggressive adduction movement.

Plyometrics and ACL Injury Prevention

Anterior cruciate ligament (ACL) tears (in the knee) are approaching near epidemic level in the sports world. Some estimates are as high as 100,000 torn ACLs per year. According to a 2001 lecture by Mike Clark, more than 30,000 of these ACL tears are believed to occur in young women who participate in sports such as soccer, basketball, and field hockey. These staggering numbers alone justify addressing ACL injury prevention in any program designed for female athletes.

A number of physical therapy and athletic training groups have begun to sell or promote programs designed for ACL injury prevention. Some are good; some are drastic oversimplifications. A sound ACL injury prevention program needs to focus on two things:

1. Single-leg strength (see chapters 6 and 7)
2. Landing and deceleration skills (described in this chapter)

Most ACL injuries occur when an athlete who is too weak attempts to land or change direction. Many studies point to female physiological predisposing characteristics such as hip structure, knee structure, or menstrual changes, but these are factors that cannot be controlled by any mortal. Coaches, athletes, therapists, or trainers cannot change the bone structure of the athlete or attempt to keep them out of competitive situations at critical points during the menstrual cycle.

The Serenity Prayer sums up one approach to ACL injury prevention:

God grant me the serenity to accept the things I cannot change,
the courage to change the things I can,
and the wisdom to know the difference.

We can obsess about why female athletes get ACL injuries more often than male athletes, but time and energy is better devoted to the things we can change. Coaches and trainers can wring their hands about the physiological predisposition of young women to ACL tears, but this will not change the facts. Girls and young women are playing sports in increasing numbers and at higher levels. What can be controlled is the development of single-leg strength, both concentric and eccentric, and landing skills, through strength training and a proper plyometric program. Plyometric training is of particular importance, but a plyometric program must be properly planned and taught. Poorly taught or poorly progressed plyometric exercises can result in patellofemoral joint problems, another area of particular concern for young female athletes. A plyometric program should always begin with the phase 1 exercises described earlier. Many of the techniques presented throughout this book are in themselves the building blocks of an ACL injury prevention program. Single-leg strength exercises, a proper plyometric program, and a conditioning program that emphasizes changes of direction go a long way toward the prevention of ACL injuries.

The development of strength cannot be overemphasized for young female athletes. They should work through the single-leg strength progression in chapter 6, from split squat to one-leg box squat, progressing to the next level only when they've mastered the previous one. Most young female athletes need weeks or even months to progress to the one-leg squat.

While young athletes are developing concentric single-leg strength through strength training, they should simultaneously be developing eccentric strength and landing skills through plyometric training. It is critical that plyometric training be properly taught and that all progression be based on competence. The four-phase progressive plyometric program described in this chapter is perfect for an ACL prevention or rehabilitation program because the initial nine weeks gradually introduce the stresses of jumping and, more important, the stresses of landing. Many plyometrics experts caution against beginning a plyometric program until the athlete has developed a high level of leg strength, but if their guidelines are followed, young athletes would never gain the benefits of plyometric training and would miss out on the vital landing skills training that the phase 1 plyometrics provide. Beginning athletes can start with beginning level plyometrics on day 1. Falling into the trap of "strength base first" only delays measures that can prevent ACL tears.

The design of the program for ACL injury prevention is simple (table 10.1). Upper-body exercises are omitted from this example but should be included if time permits. With three workouts per week, week 1 has two linear plyometric days and two days in which the athlete performs two single-leg hip and knee extension exercises. In week 2 the program is reversed to give two lateral plyometric days and two days

table 10.1

SAMPLE THREE-DAY ACL INJURY PREVENTION PROGRAM

Week 1		
Day 1	**Day 2**	**Day 3**
Linear plyometric box jump 3 × 5	Lateral plyometric Heiden and stick 3 × 5 each leg	Linear plyometric box jump 3 × 5
Split squat 3 × 8	Step-up 3 × 8 each leg	Split squat 3 × 8
Lateral squat 3 × 8	One-leg SLDL 3 × 8	Lateral squat 3 × 8
Cook hip lift 3 × 8	Hyperextension 3 × 8	Cook hip lift 3 × 8
Week 2		
Day 1	**Day 2**	**Day 3**
Lateral plyometric Heiden and stick 3 × 5 each leg	Linear plyometric box jump 3 × 5	Lateral plyometric Heiden and stick 3 × 5 each leg
Step-up 3 × 8 each leg	Split squat 3 × 8	Step-up 3 × 8 each leg
One-leg SLDL 3 × 8	Lateral squat 3 × 8	One-leg SLDL 3 × 8
Cook hip lift 3 × 8	Hyperextension 3 × 8	Cook hip lift 3 × 8

in which the athlete performs two hip extension exercises. This balances hamstring-dominant and knee-dominant work, and it balances linear and lateral jumping and landing skills. If only two workout days are available, linear and lateral plyometric days should alternate.

A progressive plyometric program is one way to improve power output. The sequence in this chapter allows you to safely improve speed, horizontal jumping ability, and vertical jumping ability while decreasing injury potential. The key is to follow the sequence and *not skip steps*. There is no shortcut to improvement, only shortcuts to injury. Plyometrics is only one of the three methods proposed for improving power. Plyometrics, medicine-ball throws (chapter 8), and Olympic lifting (chapter 11) can be successfully combined to produce great gains in power production.

Remember that more is not better. Do not exceed the recommended number of jumps or the recommended number of training days per week. Plyometrics can safely be done up to four days a week if the program is followed as described. Two linear days and two lateral days, each preceded by the corresponding warm-up (chapter 5), will not result in overuse injury if this program is followed. Athletes seeking to safely increase speed, vertical jump, overall power, or simply to prevent injury can benefit from the plyometric progressions in this chapter.

11

OLYMPIC LIFTING FOR QUICKNESS AND POWER

Every athlete is looking for the best and safest method to develop explosive power because increased power translates into a faster, more explosive athlete. Evidence continues to mount that the Olympic lifts and variations are the best method to rapidly improve power output. However, the Olympic lifts require a great deal of teaching and constant supervision. Many coaches added Olympic lifting to their programs because of the overwhelming evidence for the benefits; unfortunately, some of these coaches were not able to teach their athletes proper technique. The end result of poorly taught and unsupervised Olympic weightlifting is often injury. When injuries occur, the blame is often laid on the technique when it should be placed squarely on the coach or trainer.

If you aren't comfortable with your ability to teach the Olympic lifts, don't use them. Get your high-velocity training from medicine balls and plyometrics. The key to developing a safe and effective training program is to learn to balance theory with practicality. Before adding any explosive movements to your program, learn to perform the movements with great technique. Don't be concerned with weight—worry about technique.

Olympic lifting is great functional training. It is done standing and uses almost every muscle in the body in an explosive, coordinated fashion. Large amounts of work can be done in a short period of time after the techniques are mastered. The disadvantages are the needs to teach and coach constantly and to be concerned with technique over weight.

This chapter describes the methods I use to teach and implement the Olympic lifts in our programs. All athletes at our facility Olympic lift regardless of sport, unless they have a history of back injury. Baseball players, tennis players, and swimmers refrain from explosive overhead movements such as the snatch so as to avoid excessive stress

Olympic lifting develops power, which translates to faster, more explosive moves on the field.

on the rotator cuff. Our athletes have an injury rate near zero for supervised Olympic lifts from a position with the bar above the knees.

The easiest way to learn the Olympic lifts is from the hang position. In the hang position the bar is always kept above the knees (see figure 11.3 on page 162). This position eliminates a great deal of the lower-back stress often associated with the Olympic lifts. Any athlete can become a great technician from this position. Conversely, many athletes have difficulty learning the Olympic lifts from the floor. The physiological characteristics that make great competitive Olympic weightlifters (good biomechanical lever system, mesomorphic body type, great hip flexibility) are not possessed by most athletes. In fact, the very qualities that make good basketball players or rowers make poor competitive weightlifters. The objective is to become a better athlete in your own sport, not to become a competitive Olympic weightlifter (unless that is your sport). Olympic weightlifting should always be the means to an end, not an end itself.

The purpose of the Olympic lifts and their variations is the development of power and athleticism. Although the Olympic lifts develop impressive musculature, this should not be the primary objective. The objective is not just to move the weight but to move the weight in a fast, powerful, and athletic manner. The Olympic lifts are primarily intended to train the nervous system and secondarily develop the muscular system.

Learning the Key Olympic Lifting Positions

Following are a few guidelines for learning the Olympic lifts.

■ Think safety first. Be conscious of your surroundings. Use a lifting platform if one is available.

■ Practice proper technique. This is simple. If it doesn't look right, it probably isn't. The objective is not just to move the bar from point *a* to point *b*. The objective is to move the bar quickly and in a technically correct manner from point *a* to point *b*. Once you compromise on this point, you have failed as an Olympic lifter or a teacher of Olympic lifts.

■ Emphasize speed of movement over weight on the bar. Most of the technical mistakes made in learning the Olympic lifts are the result of one thing: *too much weight*. The battle is between ego and common sense. Your best correction is often the simplest and most obvious one: reduce the weight.

Anyone with common sense and the ability to recognize some fundamental positions can learn to clean and snatch.

There is no single right way to teach the Olympic lifts. There is, however, a simple method that I have used with great success to teach athletes in sports from football to field hockey. Remember, you are not trying to produce Olympic lifters. You are trying to make better athletes. Don't get caught up in designing a program for Olympic weightlifters; design a program for athletes to develop power using Olympic lifts and their variations.

Learning the main Olympic lifting positions is a four-step process.

Step 1: Learn the hands-free front squat. Learn the front squat before learning the clean. Start with the bar resting on the deltoids (muscles that cover the shoulders), with the arms extended out in front (figure 11.1). The hands are deliberately not on the bar. This teaches athletes to rack the bar properly and to carry the bar on the shoulders, not on the wrists. Most complaints associated with the clean result from not catching the bar properly. Don't skip this step; it is critical.

Figure 11.1 Hands-free front squat.

Step 2: Learn the clean-grip front squat. Do not use a crossover grip in the clean-grip front squat (figure 11.2). Athletes must be able to execute a proper front squat to be able to clean properly. The front squat start position is used for the clean catch and the push jerk or push press start positions.

Figure 11.2 Clean-grip front squat.

Step 3: *Learn the start position for the clean and snatch.* This is the basic pulling position. Stand with the feet shoulder-width apart, knees slightly bent, chest over the bar, hands pronated, wrists curled under, arms straight, and elbows turned out (see figure 11.3).

Figure 11.3 Clean-and-snatch start position.

Step 4: *Learn the overhead support position.* This position is used for the snatch finish, push jerk or push press finish, and overhead squat. Practice supporting the bar overhead with the arms extended. The wrists should be locked, the head slightly forward, the bar over the back of the head, and the legs bent slightly (figure 11.4).

Figure 11.4 Overhead support position.

Remember to perform all your Olympic lifts from the hang position (bar above the knees). This is a simple and safe position that can be used easily by athletes of all body dimensions. Larger, taller, or inflexible (i.e., most) athletes have difficulty learning to clean from the floor. Don't listen to so-called experts who tell you that you must clean from the floor.

Learning the Hang Clean and Close-Grip Snatch

Step 1: *Review how to pick up and put down the bar properly.* The back is arched and tight. This may seem simple, but many injuries are caused by improperly picking up and putting down the bar.

Step 2: *Review the hands-free front squat.* Learn to control the bar on the deltoids. This position *must* be learned first. Progress to a clean-grip front squat to establish flexibility in the wrists, shoulders, and elbows.

Step 3: *Review the start position.*

- Wrists curled under
- Arms straight
- Back arched
- Shoulders over the bar

Step 4: *Slide the bar down the thighs.* Think trunk flexion, not knee flexion.

Step 5a: *Perform the hang clean.* With a slightly wider than shoulder-width grip, jump, shrug, and catch in the front squat position (figure 11.5).

Figure 11.5 Hang clean.

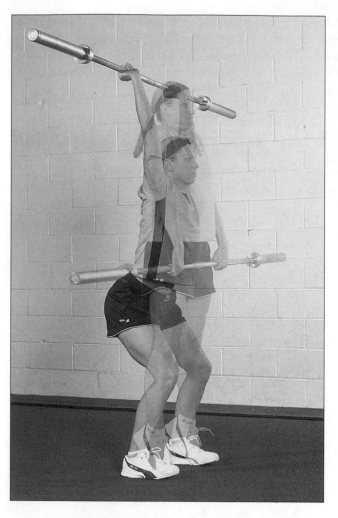

Step 5b: *Perform the close-grip snatch.* The close-grip snatch uses a grip identical to that of the clean. The wide grip generally taught for the snatch is discouraged, as its only true purpose is to allow the athlete to lift more weight. Review the overhead support position with a shoulder-width grip. Keep the bar over the back of the head, knees bent, and back arched (see figure 11.6). While executing the snatch, visualize trying to throw the bar up to hit the ceiling.

Step 6: *Return the bar properly to the blocks.* Keep the back flat and tight.

Figure 11.6 Close-grip snatch.

Teaching Cues

1. Cues for the start position

    Eyes are straight ahead.

    Chest is up.

    Back is arched.

    Arms are long and loose at the elbows.

    Wrists are curled under. This is key to keeping the bar close to the body.

    Lean out over the bar. Remember that your shoulders should be in front of the bar in the start position.

2. Cues for the pull or jump

    Jump and shrug.

    Jump and sit.

    Jump and get the elbows up (for the pull).

3. Cues for the catch (clean only)

    Sit under the bar.

    Keep the elbows up. One out of 30 athletes is actually not flexible enough to get the elbows up; 29 out of 30 say they can't.

    Hips are back.

Olympic lifting is fun, safe, and challenging when done correctly and supervised aggressively. Work on developing great technique and great bar speed, and put less emphasis on the amount of weight lifted. This process will lead to improvements in power and athleticism that you might not have thought possible.

An Alternative to Olympic Lifting

What if you don't want to lift weights but still want to make gains in lower-body power in the weight room? Jump squats may be the answer. They have been popular for years with European track-and-field athletes. Jumps squats provide a great deal of the hip power that many athletes seek from Olympic lifting and are perfect for athletes who may have reservations about technique or athletes with shoulder or back problems that prevent them from Olympic lifting.

To perform the jump squat, simply jump from a position slightly above full squat depth. Beginners can land and stabilize between jumps, and more-advanced athletes can utilize a plyometric response off the floor. An important issue for jump squats is load selection. Past guidelines recommended using a percentage (most often 25 percent) of the back squat 1RM as a load. This method of loading is extremely flawed, as it does not take into account the athlete's body weight. The following example illustrates this point.

If athlete A has a 1RM in the back squat of 500 pounds and athlete B also has a 1RM of 500 pounds, then both athletes would use 125 pounds for jumps squats using the guideline of 25 percent of back squat 1RM. Now assume that athlete A weighs 200 pounds and athlete B weighs 350 pounds. Obviously, athlete A has a strength–to–body weight ratio far superior to that of athlete B. Loading athlete A with 125 pounds may be reasonable, but athlete B, who weight 350 pounds, would probably have difficulty executing a technically sound jump squat with an additional load of 125 pounds. In fact athlete B may have difficulty performing jump squats with just body weight due to his strength–to–body weight ratio. Instead of a 1RM percentage, the following formula is suggested.

$$[(\text{Squat} + \text{body weight}) \times .4] - \text{body weight} = \text{Jump squat weight}$$

$$\text{Athlete A: } [(500 + 200) \times .4] - 200 = 80$$

$$\text{Athlete B: } [(500 + 350) \times .4] - 350 = -10$$

The example shows that the 350-pound athlete B gets sufficient loading from performing jump squats with body weight but would be overloaded by at least 125 pounds by following the simplistic 1RM percentage guideline. For athlete A, a load of 80 pounds is sufficient.

Consider the total weight that an athlete can squat as a combination of his or her body weight plus the weight on the bar, and use this number to calculate the load for jump squats. This guideline can be used by both weaker athletes looking to develop power or by larger athletes.

Whether you choose to develop your leg power through Olympic lifting or by performing jump squats, the use of external loads to train the legs and hips can be the fastest way to achieve gains in speed or jumping ability. The beauty of Olympic lifts and jump squats is that the athlete can develop power without necessarily developing large amounts of muscle. The emphasis is on the nervous system, not the muscular system, making this an excellent training method for athletes such as figure skaters, wrestlers, and gymnasts. Many athletes and coaches have the mistaken impression that explosive lifting is for football players only. This could not be further from the truth. Olympic lifting and its variations are suitable for athletes in all sports and of all sizes and should be of particular interest to athletes looking for total-body strength without increases in size.

12

PERFORMANCE ENHANCEMENT PROGRAMS

Although this chapter presents sample programs for specific sports, certain ideas must be clarified. Sport-specific strength is one of the greatest misconceptions in athletics today. The notion that each individual sport needs an individual program is flawed. Certain categories of sports have similar general needs, and the development of speed, strength, and lateral agility does not vary greatly from sport to sport. Most of the best strength and conditioning coaches in the country are actually using very similar programs to train athletes across a wide range of sports. Very rarely do coaches encounter athletes who are too strong, too fast, or too efficient in lateral movement. Is a fast baseball player in any way different from a fast football player? As a coach, would you develop speed for baseball differently from speed for football? Coaches may answer that the testing is different, but that is not the question. The *training* would probably not differ. What probably matters most is the athlete's ability to accelerate in a 10-yard area and to decelerate rapidly, not his or her ability to perform the favored test for the particular sport. The same idea applies to strength. If a baseball player wanted to get stronger, would the process be any different from that for making a football player stronger? I do not believe so. For sports like baseball, tennis, and swimming, the program might take into account the high stresses on the shoulder and thus reduce the amount of overhead lifting, but other elements would remain the same. Strength is strength. What may be more sport specific is the amount of time dedicated to the development of strength, not the methods used. There is not one way to get stronger that makes more sense for one sport than another, and there is not any one speed development program that makes more sense for one sport than another. What is important are the similarities, not the differences. This is the beauty of functional training: Usable strength and usable speed are developed in a sensible fashion.

The sample strength programs are arranged as follows: All programs begin with explosive lifts or Olympic lifts. To preserve explosiveness and to ensure perfect technique, the explosive lifts are done with three minutes' rest between sets. The explosive lifts are not done as a paired exercise. After the explosive lifts, athletes perform either two pairs of exercises or one pair of exercises and one triple set (of three exercises). These exercises are done with either one minute or one minute and 30 seconds of rest between sets.

The major sport-specific differences are not in the strength training programs but in the development of the energy systems for particular sports. Conditioning programs need to be much more sport specific than strength programs. The strength programs presented are applicable to a broad range of sports, but the conditioning programs are more specific to a single sport or group of sports.

Conditioning Programs for Improved Performance and Injury Reduction

Functional sport conditioning is constantly developing and changing. Coaches and trainers have made huge advances in their understanding of the physiology of sports and in designing programs that stress the appropriate energy systems. Although many programs now use work-to-rest ratios that are much more appropriate for team sports, few programs address changes of direction as a vital component of sport conditioning. The areas of conditioning that now need to be developed are muscular specificity and movement specificity. All the programs detailed in this chapter address changes of direction as a key component of conditioning. The ability to tolerate the muscular forces generated by accelerating and decelerating and the ability to adapt to the additional metabolic stress caused by acceleration and deceleration are the real keys to conditioning. Deficiencies in these components are often why athletes describe themselves as not being in "game shape." Most athletes have trained by running, or worse, riding a set distance in a set amount of time with no thought to the additional stresses provided by having to speed up and slow down. Athletes frequently are injured in training camp settings in spite of following a prescribed conditioning program to the letter. This is usually due to following a conditioning program that ignores the vital components of the conditioning process:

1. Acceleration
2. Deceleration
3. Change of direction

Programs that force athletes to increase speed, decrease speed, and change direction drastically reduce the incidence of early-season groin and hamstring injuries and better prepare the athletes for the demands of an actual game or event.

Conditioning programs must be sport specific in terms of these characteristics:

- *Time.* In chapter 2 we discussed analyzing the needs of a sport. Conditioning programs should not be designed to allow the athlete to pass an arbitrary conditioning test but to prepare the athlete to participate in the sport itself.

- *Movement.* Conditioning programs should incorporate changes of direction. Injuries most often occur in acceleration and deceleration. Often athletes are injured not because they are out of shape but because they are poorly prepared. One minute of straight-ahead running on a track and one minute of stop-and-start shuttle running are drastically different, both muscularly and metabolically.

- *Motor pattern.* Conditioning must incorporate the pattern of a sprint. That is, the stride pattern must be similar to sprinting. To condition the hip flexors and hamstrings (the muscles most often injured in preseason), the athlete must aggressively extend and recover the hip. Consider that a six-minute mile is run at the speed of an eight-second 40-yard dash. No wonder many athletes who think they are prepared often injure themselves.

- *Movement emphasis.* The workouts are arranged so that on lateral movement days, conditioning has a lateral movement emphasis. This means that two days per week, conditioning is done on the slide board, regardless of the sport.

Developing the Base

Our philosophy toward developing a base intentionally leaves out the term *aerobic*. As stated in chapter 2, the concept of aerobic base may be fine in the simplistic sense, but the pursuit of an aerobic base can be counterproductive. The key to any conditioning program should be to *prepare the athlete to play the sport.* Asking athletes in sprint-dominant sports (most team sports) to develop a base conditioning level through long, steady-state activity can lead to negative physiological changes at the cellular level and to muscular degradation in length, range of motion, and overuse. Athletes need to accelerate and decelerate to properly condition the muscles, and the muscles need to move in a motor pattern that is similar to the pattern used at top speed.

With this said, one obvious question is, How do you develop a base without jogging? You work backward. Instead of beginning with 30 to 40 minutes of jogging, begin with small amounts of extensive tempo running and gradually increase the amount and thus the time. Conditioning workouts initially may take only 10 minutes, but they are preceded by 20 minutes of dynamic warm-up. The end result is 30 minutes of elevated heart rate with an emphasis on dynamic flexibility and proper motor patterns. Contrast this with 30 minutes of jogging to develop the aerobic base.

Extensive tempo running is not sprinting or jogging; rather, it is periods of striding interspersed with periods of walking. Athletes stride 80 to 100 yards, depending on the facility, and walk 30 to 40 yards after each 80- to 100-yard stride. Athletes work up from 10 tempo runs to 20 and elevate the heart rate through a combination of striding and walking. Athletes never jog or revert to the short-stride motor pattern that is often implicated in loss of flexibility.

From tempo runs athletes progress to shuttle runs that emphasize acceleration, deceleration, and change of direction. Initially, 150-yard shuttle runs are done on a 50-yard course. This means that the athletes change direction only twice and accelerate and decelerate three times in each run. In week 1 the total distance is decreased drastically (from approximately 1000 yards of tempo running to 750 yards of shuttle running) to compensate for the increased muscular stress of the shuttle runs. Shuttle-run distances then are increased by either 10 to 20 percent per week (about 150 yards) or the length of the course is shortened from 50 yards to 25 yards. With the introduction of the 25-yard course, the distance either is decreased or stays the same to compensate for the increased muscular stress involved in doubling the number of changes of direction and changes in speed.

In this manner athletes can

1. develop a base while maintaining the appropriate muscle lengths and
2. develop conditioning that addresses the stops and starts that are part of so many sports.

Tempo running and shuttle running are used on linear days, whereas slide-board work is done on lateral days. The slide board is an excellent method of conditioning that meets a number of needs in all sports.

Conditioning With Slide Boards

The slide board is a training tool made popular by Olympic speedskater Eric Heiden in the 1980s. The boards are known as slide boards, stride boards, or lateral movement trainers. Speedskaters have been using the slide board for a number of years to develop skating-specific conditioning and mechanics when ice surfaces are unavailable. However, other athletes have been slow to recognize the value of the slide board as part of their off-season and preseason training. Continued improvement in slide-board design has created some durable boards that can be used by athletes at all levels. Durable boards that are adjustable from 7 feet to 10 feet are now available.

The slide board may offer the most bang for the buck of any functional conditioning tool. No other piece of equipment can do all of the following:

■ Place the athlete in a sport-specific position (for almost all sports)
■ Positively stress the abductor and adductor muscles for injury prevention
■ Allow athletes to work in groups of three to four on one piece of equipment
■ Provide functional conditioning in an interval format for three to four athletes with no adjustments (e.g., seat height) for under $500

All athletes regardless of sport (unless they are rowers) should perform lateral movement conditioning two out of four days per week. The slide board may be the best, most cost effective conditioning mode available except for actual running.

The slide board may be the most important training device available for hockey. Until the advent of the slide board, hockey players were relegated to off-season training on an exercise bike or on the track. Although both running and biking can increase aerobic capacity and anaerobic endurance, there is little similarity to the motion of skating. The slide board provides a highly hockey-specific method for doing work-capacity workouts. In addition, the slide board allows athletes to improve skating technique. Athletes can easily self-correct by placing the board in front of a large mirror and viewing their knee flexion, knee extension, and ankle extension while training.

© SportsChrome

Training with a slide board during the off-season can help hockey players improve work capacity and skating technique for in-season competition.

170

The slide board also drastically reduces all athletes' chances of incurring groin injuries in preseason. The motion of the slide board works the abductor, adductor, and hip flexor muscles, which does not occur on a bike or on any commercially available climber. In addition, the slide board works on the direct lateral pattern that is used in any change of direction and in top speedskating. When combined with a program of plyometrics and sprints, the slide board is a major tool for improving speed.

Combining the slide board with a weight vest offers another sport-specific mode of hockey and football training. Only football and ice hockey involve the additional weight of equipment as a variable in the conditioning process. For the last half of the summer conditioning program, football and hockey players at our training facility train with 10-pound weight belts on the slide board to begin to acclimate them to the weight of their sport's equipment. Some coaches minimize the impact of the equipment, but consider how different the results would be if athletes were tested in a mile run and then retested three to four days later while wearing a 10-pound weight vest or belt. Equipment weight is an important factor in some sports and should be considered in conditioning programs designed for those sports. Not adding weight to the body when conditioning for sports like hockey and football is foolish.

For football the weight vest is also included on one of the running workouts each week to simulate the weight of equipment. As a result, during the second half of summer training, football players at our training facility use the slide board twice a week with a weight vest and run once a week with the weight vest. This prepares them for the demands of football with equipment.

All soccer coaches should take the time to critically think about what makes an outstanding soccer player. Aerobic training for most soccer players, particularly young, developing players, is counterproductive. Soccer players are notorious for focusing on fitness at the expense of speed. Although this approach may appear to work at the elite level, it should be noted that elite players already have world-class speed and skills. The assumption that the fitness-over-speed approach can work with younger players is both erroneous and counterproductive.

The information in this book can help soccer players and soccer coaches develop the important skills of speed and change of direction that separate the great from the near great. Soccer players needs to develop fitness through tempo running and shuttle running, not jogging. The key to developing great soccer players is to develop sprinters, not joggers. Coaches must understand that the training does not need to look like the testing.

Sample Conditioning Programs

The sample conditioning program in table 12.1 is for an intermittent sport such as lacrosse, field hockey, ice hockey, or soccer. Days 1 and 3 have a lateral emphasis and use slide-board intervals. Days 2 and 4 have a linear emphasis and use tempo runs or shuttle runs. An additional three-day sample program for football is provided in table 12.2.

All the conditioning programs begin with extensive tempo running. Extensive tempo running involves a mixture of striding and walking. The key is to elevate the heart rate and build a base without resorting to jogging. Jogging does not involve the vigorous hip extension and corresponding sprint motor pattern that an athlete gets from tempo running and therefore is not a recommended conditioning

table 12.1

SAMPLE CONDITIONING PROGRAM FOR INTERMITTENT SPORTS (E.G., LACROSSE, FIELD HOCKEY, ICE HOCKEY, SOCCER)

	Mode	Distance or sets	Work	Rest	Treadmill	Speed (incline)	Rest	Bike	Airdyne® level M	F	Rest
Week 1											
Day 1	Slide board	5×	0:30	1:30							
Day 2	Tempo	10 × 110	0:18–0:20	0:40	10 × 0:15	10 mph (2%)	0:45	10 × 0:15	12	10	0:45
Day 3	Slide board	5×	0:30	1:30							
Day 4	Tempo	12 × 110	0:18–0:20	0:40	12 × 0:15	10 mph (2%)	0:45	12 × 0:15	12	10	0:45
Week 2											
Day 1	Slide board	6×	0:30	1:30							
Day 2	Tempo	14 × 110	0:18–0:20	0:40	14 × 0:15	11 mph (2%)	0:45	14 × 0:15	12	10	0:45
Day 3	Bike	5-mile test (record times)									
Day 4	Tempo	15 × 110	0:18–0:20	0:40	15 × 0:15	11 mph (2%)	0:45	15 × 0:15	12	10	0:45
Week 3											
Day 1	Slide board	7×	0:30	1:30							
Day 2	Run 10/10 test*					10 mph (10%)					
Day 3	Slide board	7×	0:30	1:30							
Day 4	Shuttle	5 × 150	0:25	1:35	6 × 0:30	11 mph (0%)	1:30	6 × 0:45	10	8	1:15
Week 4											
Day 1	Slide board	8×	0:30	1:30							
Day 2	Distance	2.5 miles	20:00					10 miles	L4-7	L4-7	30:00
Day 3	Slide board	8×	0:30	1:30							
Day 4	Interval	1 × 330	0:45	1:15	1 × 0:45	11 mph (2%)	1:30	2 × 0:45	10	9	1:15
		2 × 220	0:35	1:25	2 × 0:30	12.5 mph (2%)	1:30	4 × 0:30	12	10	1:30
		6 × 110	0:18	0:45	6 × 0:15	13.5 mph (2%)	0:45	6 × 0:15	15	12	0:45
Week 5											
Day 1	Slide board	6×	0:30	1:00							
Day 2	Shuttle	6 × 150	0:25	1:35	7 × 0:30	11 mph (0%)	1:30	7 × 0:45	10	8	1:15
Day 3	Bike	7-mile test (record times)									
Day 4	Distance	2.75 miles	22:00					12 miles	L4-7	L4-7	36:00

	Mode	Distance or sets	Work	Rest	Treadmill	Speed (incline)	Rest	Bike	Airdyne® level M	F	Rest
Week 6											
Day 1	Slide board	7×	0:30	1:00							
Day 2	Interval	1 × 330	0:45	1:15	1 × 0:45	11 mph (2%)	1:30	2 × 0:45	10	8	1:15
		3 × 220	0:35	1:25	3 × 0:30	12.5 mph (2%)	1:30	6 × 0:30	12	10	1:30
		5 × 110	0:18	0:45	5 × 0:15	13.5 mph (2%)	0:45	6 × 0:15	15	12	0:45
Day 3	Slide board	7×	0:30	1:00							
Day 4	Shuttle	7 × 150	0:25	1:35	8 × 0:30	11.5 mph (0%)	1:00	8 × 0:45	10	8	1:15
Week 7											
Day 1	Slide board	8×	0:30	1:00							
Day 2	Distance	3 miles	24:00					14 miles	L4-7	L4-7	42:00
Day 3	Slide board	8×	0:30	1:00							
Day 4	Interval	2 × 330	0:45	1:15	2 × 0:45	11.5 mph (2%)	1:30	2 × 0:45	10	8	1:15
		3 × 220	0:35	1:25	3 × 0:30	13 mph (2%)	1:30	6 × 0:30	12	10	1:30
		3 × 110	0:18	0:45	3 × 0:15	14 mph (2%)	0:45	8 × 0:15	15	12	0:45
Week 8											
Day 1	Slide board	9×	0:30	1:00							
Day 2	Shuttle	1 × 300	1:05	2:00	1 × 1:00	10.5 mph (2%)	1:00	4 × 0.5 mile	10	8	3:00
		6 × 150	0:25	1:35	6 × 0:30	11.5 mph (2%)	1:30				
Day 3	Bike	10-mile test (record times)									
Day 4	Distance	4 miles	30:00					15 miles	L4-7	L4-7	45:00
Week 9											
Day 1	Slide board	10×	0:30	1:00							
Day 2	Interval	4 × 220	0:35	1:25	4 × 0:30	12.5 mph (2%)	1:00	3 × 0:45	10	8	1:15
		8 × 110	0:18	0:45	8 × 0:15	13.5 mph (2%)	0:45	6 × 0:30	12	10	1:30
								5 × 0:15	15	12	0:45
Day 3	Slide board	10×	0:30	1:00							
Day 4	Shuttle	2 × 300	1:05	2:00	2 × 1:00	10.5 mph (2%)	1:00	5 × 0.5 mile	10	8	3:00
		5 × 150	0:25	1:35	5 × 0:30	11.5 mph (2%)	1:00				

(continued)

table 12.1 (continued)

	Mode	Distance or sets	Work	Rest	Treadmill	Speed (incline)	Rest	Bike	Airdyne® level M	F	Rest
Week 10											
Day 1	Slide board	7×, with 10 lb	0:30	1:00							
Day 2	Distance	4 miles	30:00					15 miles	L4-7	L4-7	43:00
Day 3	10/10 test*					10 mph (10%)					
Day 4	Interval	5 × 220	0:35	1:25	5 × 0:30	12.5 mph (2%)	1:00	3 × 0:45	10	8	1:15
		7 × 110	0:18	0:45	7 × 0:15	13.5 mph (2%)	0:45	7 × 0:30	12	10	1:30
								5 × 0:15	15	12	0:45
Week 11											
Day 1	Slide board	8×, with 10 lb	0:30	1:00							
Day 2	Shuttle	3 × 300	1:05	2:00	3 × 1:00	10.5 mph (2%)	1:00	2 × 1 mile	9	7	5:00
		4 × 150	0:25	1:35	4 × 0:30	11.5 mph (2%)	1:00	1 × 0.5 mile	10	8	
Day 3	Bike	10-mile test (record times)									
Day 4	Distance	4 miles	30:00					15 miles	L4-7	L4-7	42:00
Week 12											
Day 1	Slide board	8×, with 10 lb	0:30	1:00							
Day 2	Interval	5 × 220	0:35	1:25	5 × 0:30	12.5 mph (2%)	1:00	3 × 0:45	10	8	1:15
		8 × 110	0:18	0:45	8 × 0:15	13.5 mph (2%)	0:45	7 × 0:30	12	10	1:30
								7 × 0:15	15	12	0:45
Day 3	Slide board	8×, with 10 lb	0:30	1:00							
Day 4	Shuttle	4 × 300	1:05	2:00	3 × 1:00	10 mph (2%)	1:00	2 × 1 mile	9	7	5:00
		3 × 150	0:25	1:35	5 × 0:30	11 mph (2%)	1:00	2 × 0.5 mile	10	8	3:00

*The run 10/10 test is a run to near failure at 10% incline and 10 mph.

table 12.2

SAMPLE CONDITIONING PROGRAM FOR FOOTBALL

	All positions	Line	Skill	Rest
Week 1				
Monday	Tempo run—stride 100 yards, walk end zone (× 8)			
	Total time should be less than 8 min., end zone walk is the rest time			
Tuesday	20 shuttle × 3	60 shuttle × 6 (0:15)	60 shuttle × 6 (0:13)	0:45
	Slide board after run 6 × 0:15-0:45			
Thursday	Tempo run—stride 100 yards, walk end zone (× 8) (less than 8 min.)			
Friday	Slide board 6 × 0:15-0:45			
Week 2				
Monday	Tempo run—stride 100 yards, walk end zone (× 10) (less than 10 min.)			
Tuesday	20 shuttle × 3	60 shuttle × 7 (0:15)	60 shuttle × 7 (0:13)	0:45
	Slide board after run 7 × 0:15-0:45			
Thursday	Tempo run—stride 100 yards, walk end zone (× 10) (less than 10 min.)			
Friday	Slide board 8 × 0:15-0:45			
Week 3				
Monday	Tempo run—stride 100 yards, walk end zone (× 12) (less than 12 min.)			
Tuesday	20 shuttle × 3	60 shuttle × 8 (0:15)	60 shuttle × 8 (0:13)	0:45
	Slide board after run 8 × 0:15-0:45			
Thursday	Tempo run—stride 100 yards, walk end zone (× 12) (less than 12 min.)			
Friday	Slide board 10 × 0:15-0:45			
Week 4				
Monday		12 × 55 (9 sec)	12 × 55 (7.5 sec)	
Tuesday	20 shuttle × 3	60 shuttle × 9 (0:15)	60 shuttle × 9 (0:13)	0:45
	Slide board after run 9 × 0:15-0:45			
Thursday	Tempo run—stride 100 yards, walk end zone (× 12) (less than 12 min.)			
Friday	Slide board 10 × 0:15-0:45			
Week 5				
Monday		14 × 55 (9 sec)	14 × 55 (7.5 sec)	
Tuesday	20 shuttle × 3	60 shuttle × 10 (0:15)	60 shuttle × 10 (0:13)	0:45
	Slide board after run 8 × 0:15-0:45			
Thursday	150 shuttle × 5 (line 0:33) (skill 0:30)			
	50-yard course			
Friday	Slide board 11 × 0:15-0:45			
Week 6				
Monday		16 × 55 (9 sec)	16 × 55 (7.5 sec)	
Tuesday	20 shuttle × 4	60 shuttle × 11 (0:15)	60 shuttle × 11 (0:13)	0:45
	Slide board after run 8 × 0:15-0:45			

(continued)

175

table 12.2 (*continued*)

	All positions	**Line**	**Skill**	**Rest**
Week 6 *(continued)*				
Thursday	150 shuttle × 5 (line 0:35) (skill 0:30) 25-yard course.			
Friday	Slide board 11 × 0:15-0:45			
Week 7				
Monday		18 × 55 (9 sec)	18 × 55 (7.5 sec)	
Tuesday	20 shuttle × 5	60 shuttle × 12 (0:15)	60 shuttle × 12 (0:13)	0:45
	Slide board after run 12 × 0:15-0:45			
Thursday	150 shuttle × 6 (line 0:33) (skill 0:30) 50-yard course			
Friday	Slide board 12 × 0:15-0:45			
Week 8	**Light lifting week, easy run Thursday**			
Monday		14 × 55 (9 sec)	14 × 55 (7.5 sec)	
Tuesday	20 shuttle × 3	60 shuttle × 8 (0:15)	60 shuttle × 8 (0:13)	0:45
	Slide board after run 8 × 0:15-0:45			
Thursday	Tempo run—stride 100 yards, walk end zone × 8			
Friday	Slide board 10 × 0:15-0:45			
Week 9				
Monday		18 × 55 (9 sec)	18 × 55 (7.5 sec)	
Tuesday	20 shuttle × 3	60 shuttle × 12 (0:15)	60 shuttle × 12 (0:13)	0:45
	Slide board after run 12 × 0:15-0:45			
Thursday	150 shuttle × 6 (line 0:33) (skill 0:30) 25-yard course			
Friday	Slide board 12 × 0:15-0:45			
Week 10				
Monday		20 × 55 (9 sec)	20 × 55 (7.5 sec)	
Tuesday	20 shuttle × 3	60 shuttle × 12 (0:15)	60 shuttle × 12 (0:13)	0:45
	Slide board after run 12 × 0:15-0:45			
Thursday	150 shuttle × 7 (line 0:33) (skill 0:30) 50-yard course			
Friday	Slide board 14 × 0:15-0:45			
Week 11				
Monday		22 × 55 (9 sec)	22 × 55 (7.5 sec)	
Tuesday	20 shuttle × 3	60 shuttle × 14 (0:15)	60 shuttle × 14 (0:13)	0:45
	Slide board after run 12 × 0:15-0:45			
Thursday	150 shuttle × 7 (line 0:33) (skill 0:30) 25-yard course			
Friday	Slide board 15 × 0:15-0:45			

	All positions	Line	Skill	Rest
Week 12				
Monday		20 × 55 (9 sec)	20 × 55 (7.5 sec)	
Tuesday	20 shuttle × 3	60 shuttle × 12 (0:15)	60 shuttle × 12 (0:13)	0:45
	Slide board after run 12 × 0:15-0:45			
Thursday	Tempo run—stride 100 yards, walk end zone (× 12)			
Friday	Off			

method. Remember, you are trying to condition both the muscles and the circulatory system.

The program provides three different workout options on linear days (days 2 and 4). One workout option is running outdoors, one is treadmill running, and a third option is cycling on a stationary bike. The cycle workout is for injured athletes only. We do not recommend cycling for healthy athletes. Shuttle workouts are change-of-direction workouts. This means that the distance is run in either 25- or 50-yard intervals.

Most sports have far more similarities than differences. There are obvious differences, but what most sports have in common are the key skills of acceleration, deceleration, and change of direction. Whether you are a football player or a figure skater, these skills are critical. To improve conditioning while reducing the chance of injury, acceleration, deceleration, and change of direction must be incorporated into the conditioning program. In addition, you must think outside the box. Slide boards and weight vests are two not-so-obvious tools that help make conditioning programs that are both sport specific and, more important, movement specific.

Sample Performance Enhancement Programs

In keeping with the concept of sports-general programming, I do not present most programs by sport but rather focus on the unique aspects of certain groups of sports. For example, the baseball, tennis, and swimming programs have a decreased emphasis on overhead activities so as not to overstress the already well-worked rotator cuff muscles. Sports such as soccer that do not require as much absolute strength can use two-day or three-day lifting programs, while football almost universally uses a four-day program.

Two-Day Programs

Two-day programs are the most difficult to design. Two-day programs are generally used in-season or in sports that do not require a lot of absolute strength. I recommend two-day programs only for in-season workouts. The minimum recommended time to allot to the strength program for any sport is three days per week in the off-season. Please note that all programs should be preceded by a thorough dynamic warm-up session and at least 12 to 15 minutes of torso training. In addition, I recommend 12 to 20 minutes of conditioning before or after the workout. One and a half to two hours must be allocated to each training session to include warm-up, torso work, strength work, and postworkout stretching or soft-tissue work.

The difficulty with two-day programs is attempting to train all of the 10 essential areas in only two sessions. For two-day programs, compromises must be made. These are the 10 essential components of the strength program:

1. Knee-dominant hip and leg pushing exercises—generally squatting (see chapter 6).

2. Single-leg knee-dominant hip and leg pushing exercises—one-leg squats and variations (see chapter 6).

3. Straight-leg hip extension—straight-leg deadlifts, modified straight-leg deadlifts, hyperextensions, and single-leg variations (see chapter 7).

4. Bent-leg hip extension—hip lift variations and stability-ball hip extensions (see chapter 7).

5. Torso work—also called core work or ab work (see chapter 8).

6. Supine presses—such as the bench press (see chapter 9).

7. Overhead presses—such as dumbbell or bar military presses (see chapter 9).

8. Horizontal pulls—such as rows (see chapter 9).

9. Vertical pull—chin-ups and variations (see chapter 9).

10. Explosive power development—most often Olympic lifts, but plyometric work or jump squats can be substituted (see chapters 10 and 11).

The key to a properly designed functional training program is combining these categories without overemphasizing or underemphasizing any particular component. In a two-day workout, a combination Olympic movement such as a clean and front squat combination or a clean and push jerk combination works two areas (explosive power plus hip and leg push, or explosive power and overhead press) in one exercise. In addition, incline presses can be used as a compromise between supine pressing and overhead pressing. For a combo vertical and horizontal pull, try sternum chin-ups or V-grip chin-ups, as these combine a chin-up action with a rowing type of movement. See tables 12.3, 12.4, and 12.5 for two-day workout guidelines and samples.

table 12.3

SAMPLE TWO-DAY LIFTING WORKOUT

Day 1 Explosive/Olympic	Day 2 Explosive/Olympic
Pair 1	
Hip/leg push	One-leg hip/leg push
Supine press (chest emphasis)	High incline press (deltoid emphasis)
Pair 2	
Pull-up/chin-up	Row
Bent-leg hip extension	Straight-leg hip extension

table 12.4

SAMPLE TWO-DAY PROGRAM: ANY SPORT EXCEPT BASEBALL, SWIMMING, OR TENNIS

Name	Bench	Squat	Clean	Body weight	Pull-up
John Doe	290	370	300	200	20

Day 1	Tempo	Rest	Week 1	Week 2	Week 3
Warm-up and abs					
Snatch	Explosive	3 min.	135 × 5	135 × 5	135 × 5
			142.5 × 5	142.5 × 5	142.5 × 5
			142.5 × 5	150 × 5	157.5 × 5
			142.5 × 5	142.5 × 5	142.5 × 5
Chin-up	2/0/2	1 min.	BW × 10	10 × 10	15 × 10
			BW × 10	10 × 10	15 × 10
			BW × 10	10 × 10	15 × 10
pair with	2/0/Exp		185 × 10	185 × 10	185 × 10
			190 × 10	195 × 10	203.5 × 10
Front squat			180 × 10	190 × 10	195 × 10
Parallel grip dumbbell bench	2/0/2	1 min.	92.8 × 10	95.7 × 10	98.6 × 10
			92.8 × 10	95.7 × 10	98.6 × 10
			92.8 × 10	95.7 × 10	98.6 × 10
pair with	2/0/2		22.5 × 10	26.25 × 10	30 × 10
			22.5 × 10	26.25 × 10	30 × 10
One-leg SLDL			22.5 × 10	26.25 × 10	30 × 10

Day 2	Tempo	Rest	Week 1	Week 2	Week 3
Warm-up and abs					
Clean	Explosive	3 min.	210 × 5	210 × 5	225 × 5
			232.5 × 5	232.5 × 5	240 × 5
			232.5 × 5	240 × 5	247.5 × 5
			232.5 × 5	232.5 × 5	240 × 5
Sternum chin-up	2/0/2	1 min.	BW × 10	10 × 10	15 × 10
			BW × 10	10 × 10	15 × 10
pair with			BW × 10	10 × 10	15 × 10
			185 × 10	185 × 10	185 × 10
Balance board front squat			185 × 10	194.25 × 10	203.5 × 10
			185 × 10	185 × 10	185 × 10

(continued)

table 12.4 *(continued)*

Day 2 *(continued)*	Tempo	Rest	Week 1	Week 2	Week 3
Bench (3 down, 1 sec pause)	3/1/Exp	1 min.	203 × 10	203 × 10	203 × 10
			210.3 × 10	217.5 × 10	224.75 × 10
pair with			210.3 × 10	210.25 × 10	217.5 × 10
			209.5 × 10	203 × 10	210.25 × 10
	2/0/2		× 8	× 10	× 12
Ball leg curl			× 8	× 10	× 12
			× 8	× 10	× 12

Note: All of the workouts shown are copies of spreadsheets. John Doe's max weights are the key data that allow the sheet to calculate bench max, squat max, and so on. These max weights are only relevant in that they produce the actual spreadsheet numbers.

To use the chart, simply read across from left to right. Perform the lift listed at the tempo described, with the given weight and number of reps.

table 12.5

SAMPLE TWO-DAY PROGRAM: BASEBALL, SWIMMING, TENNIS

Name	Bench	Squat	Clean	Body weight	Pull-up
John Doe	290	370	275	200	20

Day 1	Tempo	Rest	Week 1	Week 2	Week 3
Warm-up and abs					
Light clean	Explosive	3 min.	135 × 5	135 × 5	135 × 5
			185 × 5	190 × 5	185 × 5
			185 × 5	185 × 5	195 × 5
			175 × 5	175 × 5	185 × 5
Chin-up	2/0/2	1 min.	BW × 10	10 × 10	15 × 10
			BW × 10	10 × 10	15 × 10
pair with			BW × 10	10 × 10	15 × 10
	2/0/Exp		185 × 10	185 × 10	185 × 10
			190 × 10	195 × 10	203.5 × 10
Front squat			180 × 10	190 × 10	195 × 10
Parallel grip dumbbell bench	2/0/2	1 min.	92.8 × 10	95.7 × 10	98.6 × 10
			92.8 × 10	95.7 × 10	98.6 × 10
pair with			92.8 × 10	95.7 × 10	98.6 × 10
	2/0/2		22.5 × 10	26.25 × 10	30 × 10
One-leg SLDL			22.5 × 10	26.25 × 10	30 × 10
			22.5 × 10	26.25 × 10	30 × 10

Day 2	Tempo	Rest	Week 1	Week 2	Week 3
Warm-up and abs					
Clean	Explosive	4 min.	210 × 5	210 × 5	225 × 5
			232.5 × 5	232.5 × 5	240 × 5
			232.5 × 5	240 × 5	247.5 × 5
			232.5 × 5	232.5 × 5	240 × 5
Sternum chin-up	Explosive	1 min.	BW × 10	10 × 10	15 × 10
			BW × 10	10 × 10	15 × 10
pair with			BW × 10	10 × 10	15 × 10
	Explosive		185 × 10	185 × 10	185 × 10
Balance board front squat			185 × 10	194.25 × 10	203.5 × 10
			185 × 10	185 × 10	185 × 10
Bench (3 down, 1 sec. pause)	3/1/Exp		203 × 10	203 × 10	203 × 10
			210.3 × 10	217.5 × 10	224.75 × 10
pair with			210.3 × 10	210.25 × 10	217.5 × 10
			209.5 × 10	203 × 10	210.25 × 10
	2/0/2		× 8	× 10	× 12
Ball leg curl			× 8	× 10	× 12
			× 8	× 10	× 12

The primary difference between this program and the one in table 12.4 is that explosive overhead lifts have been eliminated.

Three-Day Programs

Three-day programs are much easier to design than two-day programs because you have 50 percent more training time. Three days is the minimum time recommended for most off-season training programs. The exceptions are programs for athletes who have less need for absolute strength or athletes such as figure skaters, gymnasts, and swimmers who already devote a large part of their time to training and would have difficulty complying with a three-day program. In most team sports, three days should be considered the minimum amount of training.

In a three-day program it is easier to balance the 10 key components. Fewer compromises are needed in a three-day program, although some are still necessary. For instance, it may be possible to row only once per week in a three-day program, although chin-ups can be performed twice. In three-day programs, athletes still begin with an explosive exercise every day and perform a primary pair followed by a triple set.

table 12.6

SAMPLE THREE-DAY EXPLOSIVE/OLYMPIC LIFTING WORKOUT

Day 1 Explosive/Olympic	Day 2 Explosive/Olympic	Day 3 Explosive/Olympic
Pair Hip/leg push Supine press	Incline press One-leg hip/leg push	Hip/leg push Incline press (combo supine + overhead press)
Tri set One-leg hip/leg push Overhead press Vertical pull (pull-up/chin-up)	Overhead press Hip extension (bent leg) Horizontal pull (row)	Hip extension Horizontal or vertical pull (row or chin-up) One-leg hip/leg push

table 12.7

SAMPLE THREE-DAY PROGRAM

Name	Bench	Squat	Clean	Body weight	Pull-up
John Doe	195	180	190	173	13

Day 1	Tempo	Rest	Week 1	Week 2	Week 3
Warm-up and abs					
Clean	Explosive	4 min.	143 × 5	143 × 5	143 × 5
			143 × 5	143 × 5	143 × 5
			143 × 5	143 × 5	143 × 5
Chin-up *pair with*	2/0/2	1:30 min.	BW × 8	BW × 8	BW × 8
			7 × 8	13 × 8	16 × 8
			7 × 8	7 × 8	13 × 8
Front box squat	2/0/Exp		BW × 8	BW × 8	BW × 8
			BW × 8	BW × 8	BW × 8
				BW × 8	BW × 8

Day 1 (continued)	Tempo	Rest	Week 1	Week 2	Week 3
Dumbbell incline tri set	2/0/2	1 min.	47 × 8	49 × 8	51 × 8
			47 × 8	49 × 8	51 × 8
				49 × 8	51 × 8
with	2/0/Exp		× 10	× 15	× 20
Hyperextensions			× 10	× 15	× 20
				× 15	× 20
and			× 8	× 10	× 12
Overhead split squat			× 8	× 10	× 12
				× 10	× 12

Day 2	Tempo	Rest	Week 1	Week 2	Week 3
Warm-up and abs					
Dumbbell snatch (thrower's one-arm)	Explosive	4 min.	48 × 5	48 × 5	48 × 5
			48 × 5	50 × 5	50 × 5
			48 × 5	50 × 5	50 × 5
Bench (3 down, 1 sec pause)	2/0/Exp	1:30	117 × 8	117 × 8	117 × 8
			141 × 8	146 × 8	146 × 8
pair with			137 × 8	137 × 8	137 × 8
One-leg bench squat *or* **split squat**	2/0/2		× 8	× 8	× 8
			× 8	× 8	× 8
				× 8	× 8
Dumbbell row tri set	2/0/Exp	1 min.	× 8	× 8	× 8
			× 8	× 8	× 8
with				× 8	× 8
Straight-leg deadlift	2/0/2		× 8	× 10	× 10
			× 8	× 10	× 10
				× 10	× 10
and	2/0/2		× 8	× 8	× 8
Alternate dumbbell press			× 8	× 8	× 8
				× 8	× 8

Day 3	Tempo	Rest	Week 1	Week 2	Week 3
Warm-up and abs					
High hang clean	Explosive	4 min.	143 × 5	143 × 5	143 × 5
			143 × 5	143 × 5	143 × 5
			143 × 5	143 × 5	143 × 5

(continued)

table 12.7 *(continued)*

Day 3 *(continued)*	Tempo	Rest	Week 1	Week 2	Week 3
Chin-up	2/0/Exp	1:30	BW × 8	BW × 8	BW × 8
			BW × 8	BW × 8	BW × 8
pair with				BW × 8	BW × 8
Front box squat			BW × 8	BW × 8	BW × 8
			BW × 8	BW × 8	BW × 8
				BW × 8	BW × 8
Overhead split squat tri set	2/0/Exp		× 8	× 10	× 12
			× 8	× 10	× 12
with				× 10	× 12
Push-up/scapula push-up	2/0/2		8 + 8	× 10	× 12
			8 + 8	× 10	× 12
and				× 10	× 12
	2/0/2		× 8	× 10	× 12
			× 8	× 10	× 12
Ball hip with roller				× 10	× 12

Four-Day Programs

Four-day programs are preferred for off-season training for most sports. Four-day workouts permit combining all the elements needed for strength development and for speed and conditioning. In a four-day program, few compromises are necessary to address all the critical variables. The four-day workout allows inclusion of additional torso work or rehabilitation or "prehabilitation" exercises that might not fit into a two- or three-day workout.

Some weighted torso work or work requiring specialized equipment such as cable columns or hyper benches may be included in the workout instead of before lifting.

In the four-day program in table 12.8, leg work is done every day, but the emphasis switches from knee-dominant to hip-dominant work each day. (Although exercises such as lunges and step-ups are good hamstring exercises, here they are considered hip and leg push exercises due to the combination of hip extension and knee extension.)

table 12.8

SAMPLE FOUR-DAY EXPLOSIVE/OLYMPIC LIFTING WORKOUT

Day 1 Explosive/Olympic	Day 2 Explosive/Olympic	Day 3 Explosive/Olympic	Day 4 Explosive/Olympic
Pair			
Hip/leg push	Supine press	Hip/leg push	Incline press
Vertical pull (pull-up/chin-up)	Straight-leg hip extension	Vertical pull (pull-up/chin-up)	Straight-leg hip extension
Tri set			
One-leg hip/leg push	Overhead press (shoulder)	One-leg hip/leg push	Overhead press (shoulder)
Horizontal pull (row)		Horizontal pull (row)	Bent-leg hip extension
Chop-lift-OBO	Bent-leg hip extension	Chop-lift-OBO	Shoulder circuit
	Shoulder circuit		

OBO = off-bench oblique.

table 12.9

SAMPLE FOUR-DAY PROGRAM

Name	Bench	Squat	Clean	Body weight	Pull-up
John Doe	105	100	85	135	5

Day 1	Tempo	Rest	Week 1	Week 2	Week 3
Warm-up and abs					
Dumbbell snatch	Explosive	4 min.	21 × 5	22 × 5	23 × 5
			21 × 5	22 × 5	23 × 5
			21 × 5	22 × 5	23 × 5
				22 × 5	23 × 5
12-in. chin-up	2/0/2	1 min.	BW × 8	BW × 8	BW × 8
			3 × 8	4 × 8	5 × 8
pair with				3 × 8	4 × 8
				3 × 8	3 × 8
Front box squat	2/0/Exp	1 min.	60 × 8	60 × 8	60 × 8
			73 × 8	75 × 8	78 × max
				73 × 8	75 × 8
					73 × 8

(continued)

185

table 12.9 *(continued)*

Day 1 *(continued)*	Tempo	Rest	Week 1	Week 2	Week 3
Dumbbell row tri set	2/0/2	1 min.	× 8	× 8	× 8
with			× 8	× 8	× 8
				× 8	× 8
Split squat	2/0/Exp	1 min.	11 × 8	13 × 8	14 × 8
and			11 × 8	13 × 8	14 × 8
				13 × 8	14 × 8
Standing lift			× 10	× 10	× 10
			× 10	× 10	× 10
				× 10	× 10

Day 2	Tempo	Rest	Week 1	Week 2	Week 3
Warm-up and abs					
Clean	Explosive	4 min.	64 × 5	64 × 5	64 × 5
			65 × 5	68 × 5	68 × 5
			65 × 5	68 × 5	72 × max
				65 × 5	68 × 5
Dumbbell bench	2/0/Exp	1 min.	15 × 8	17.5 × 8	20 × 20
pair with			15 × 8	17.5 × 8	
				17.5 × 8	
Ball hip extension with roller	2/0/2	1 min.	× 8	× 10	× 12
			× 8	× 10	× 12
				× 10	× 12
Weighted dip + scapula dip	2/0/Exp	1 min.	BW × 8 + 8	BW × 8 + 8	BW × 8 + 8
pair with			BW × 8 + 8	19 × 8 + 8	23 × 8 + 8
				19 × 8 + 8	23 × 8 + 8
Hammer curl	2/0/2	1 min.	× 8	× 8	× 8
			× 8	× 8	× 8
and				× 8	× 8
Standing chop			× 10	× 10	× 10
			× 10	× 10	× 10
				× 10	× 10

Day 3	Tempo	Rest	Week 1	Week 2	Week 3
Warm-up and abs					
Alternate dumbbell push jerk	Explosive	4 min.	23.1 × 5	24.2 × 5	25.2 × 5
			23.1 × 5	24.2 × 5	25.2 × 5
			23.1 × 5	24.2 × 5	25.2 × 5
				24.2 × 5	25.2 × 5

Day 3 (continued)	Tempo	Rest	Week 1	Week 2	Week 3
Balance board squat	3/0/Exp	1 min.	43 × 8	45 × 8	47 × 8
			43 × 8	45 × 8	47 × 8
pair with				45 × 8	47 × 8
Parallel grip chin-up	2/0/2	1 min.	BW × 8	BW × 8	BW × 8
			3 × 8	3.8 × 8	5 × 8
				2.5 × 8	4 × 8
				2.5 × 8	3 × 8
Lateral squat tri set	2/0/2	1 min.	22.5 × 8	25 × 8	27 × 8
with			22.5 × 8	25 × 8	27 × 8
				25 × 8	27 × 8
Upper back dumbbell row	2/0/1	1 min.	× 8	× 8	× 8
and			× 8	× 8	× 8
Standing lift			× 10	× 10	× 10
			× 10	× 10	× 10
				× 10	× 10

Day 4	Tempo	Rest	Week 1	Week 2	Week 3
Warm-up and abs					
Light clean	Explosive	4 min.	59.5 × 5	59.5 × 5	59.5 × 5
			59.5 × 5	61.6 × 5	61.6 × 5
			59.5 × 5	59.5 × 5	63.75 × 5
				59.5 × 5	59.5 × 5
Core board rotational push-up	2/0/Exp	1 min.	× 12	× 14	× 16
			× 12	× 14	× 16
pair with				× 14	× 16
Stability ball leg curl with roller	2/0/2	1 min.	× 8	× 10	× 12
			× 8	× 10	× 12
				× 10	× 12
External rotation tri set	2/0/2	1 min.	6.3 × 8	7.4 × 8	8.4 × 8
with			6.3 × 8	7.4 × 8	8.4 × 8
				7.4 × 8	8.4 × 8
Hip circuit (SL, BL, AB, internal rotation)	2/0/2	1 min.	× 8	× 10	× 12
			× 8	× 10	× 12
and			× 10	× 10	× 10
Standing chop			× 10	× 10	× 10
			× 10	× 10	× 10

Program design is the culmination of all you have learned throughout this book about functional training. Programs should be designed with some simple concepts in mind:

- Begin with body weight when practical.
- Develop technique on stable surfaces before progressing to unstable surfaces.
- Design a program that can be completed in the allotted time. Think about how long each set will take and how much rest to allow between sets. A good guideline is about 16 to 20 sets in a one-hour workout.
- Design a workout that addresses all 10 key components, or as many as practical in the time available.
- Design a workout that prepares an athlete to play a sport, not a workout that mimics one of the strength sports (bodybuilding, power lifting, Olympic lifting). Simulating a strength sport may be the largest mistake in program design.

Good program design takes time and thought. Don't waste valuable time with valueless exercises. Always go for the most bang for the buck. Most single-joint exercises do not work a movement pattern but instead work one joint action in one plane. Exercise such as lunges and split squats can be used to develop single-leg strength, balance, and flexibility. This three-pronged benefit is the key to good exercise selection.

references

Cook, G. 1997. Functional training for the torso. *NSCA Journal* (April): 14-19.

Francis, C. 2000. *Training for speed*. Canberra, Australia: Faccioni Speed and Conditioning Consultant.

Gambetta, V. 1995. *Straight ahead speed*. Videocassette. Sarasota, FL: Gambetta Sports Systems. Cranston, RI: Distributed by MF Athletic.

Gambetta, V., and G. Gray. 2002. *Following the functional path*. [Online]. Available: www.gambetta.com/a97004p.html [January 28, 2003].

McGill, S. 2002. *Low back disorders*. Champaign, IL: Human Kinetics.

Richardson, C., G. Jull, P. Hodges, and J. Hides. 1999. *Therapeutic exercise for spinal segmental stabilization in low back pain*. London: Churchill Livingston.

Watkins, R. (Ed). 1996. *The spine in sports*. St. Louis, MO: Mosby. 283-302.

Note: The italicized *f* or *t* following a page number denote a figure or table on that page, respectfully. The italicized *ff* or *tt* following a page number denotes multiple figures or tables on that page.

Mike Boyle is regarded as a leader in the field of strength and conditioning. He is director of performance for Athletes' Performance Los Angeles, located at the Home Depot Center in Carson, California.

Before his work at Athletes' Performance, Boyle was owner of Mike Boyle Strength and Conditioning, providing performance enhancement and injury prevention to athletes of all ages. He also spent 17 years as the strength and conditioning coach at Boston University and 10 years as the strength and conditioning coach for the NHL's Boston Bruins. He was one of the first strength and conditioning coaches to prepare athletes specifically for the NFL Combine, a trend that is now industry-wide. He also was the strength and conditioning coach for the 1998 gold medal-winning U.S. women's Olympic ice hockey team.

Widely known for his work with hockey players, Boyle also has trained athletes in many of the major professional sports leagues in North America, including the NHL, NFL, NBA, MLB, MLS, and WNBA.

In addition, Boyle has produced eight videos, available from MF Athletic at 1-800-556-7464 or www.performbetter.com.

Boyle lives in El Segundo, California, with his wife, Cynthia. He can be reached at mboyle@athletesperformance.com.

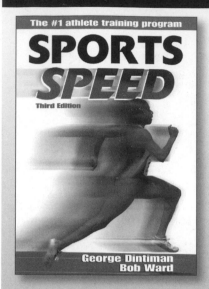